D1420156

AFTER THE MANIFESTO

WRITING, ARCHITECTURE, AND MEDIA IN A NEW CENTURY

—

EDITED BY
CRAIG BUCKLEY

GSAPP BOOKS   T6) EDICIONES

AFTER THE MANIFESTO

CRAIG BUCKLEY

THERE HAS BEEN SOMETHING LIKE A MANIA for the manifesto in recent years. While only a little while ago one could still hear about the absence of manifestos in architecture, today we seem to be surrounded by them. Manifestos have been the subject of public reading marathons, taken up as themes for biennales, exhibited at galleries, exchanged for drinks, and become the subject of conferences at schools of architecture.[1] About this resurgence, there is understandably little consensus. The urgency of the genre has returned to prominence at a moment of economic crisis and political protests over inequality, but it also appears wedded ever more intimately to official institutions of culture, which have gravitated toward performative genres in recent years. For some, the manifesto remains an archaism, the product of another century whose current revival artfully masks the fact that it has outlived its use. For others, the manifesto remains protean, a form that not only continues to remake itself but also stands to be reclaimed in our age of rapidly changing media. For still others, it is precisely the outmoded, untimely qualities of the manifesto that make it so interesting at present. What does this confusing situation imply about the ongoing relevance of the manifesto form today?

 After the Manifesto wrestles with such questions by bringing together a series of reflections on the history of the form in architectural culture. In looking back, rather than forward, *After the Manifesto* could be seen to betray the very future-oriented nature of the genre, which has vividly projected the outlines of non-extant forms, movements, and figures, and has often succeeded in bringing some version of them into the world. On the one hand, *After the Manifesto* registers a palpable feeling that however actual and contemporary, the manifesto form represents the legacy of a different historical moment. To think about the manifesto today is to think about where one stands relative to the boldest claims made by architects over the last century. Yet the title of the book can be understood in another sense as well, less as a time that comes after manifestos than as an interest in their *aftereffects*; the affirmations and rejections, replications and repressions, debates and silences, misunderstandings and recuperations that manifestos set in motion. A manifesto, after all, is a text that calls for a response, even if it is not always the one expected or desired by its authors. Paradoxically, then, while manifestos have often served as vehicles for making absolute claims, they themselves are anything but. The manifesto is a form colored and remade according to its time. A key rhetorical weapon deployed by the historical avant-gardes, the manifesto's language of rupture and revolution was an indispensable vehicle for setting transformative architectural projects in motion. At the same time, manifestos have also been associated with some of the more problematic elements of such vanguard positioning, from hyperbole, exhortation, and naïveté to misogyny, racism, and sympathies for fascism. How, if at all, do these conflicting legacies bear on the manifesto's contemporary resurgence? To what extent has the genre reformulated itself, adopting different qualities and addressing other purposes today? Can the manifestos of the twenty-first century still be recognized using the terms of the past?

While one may feel increasingly swamped by manifestos, it is also true that we remain largely ignorant about the state of the architectural manifesto in recent decades. Although a few texts have been preserved in collections of architectural culture and theory, no systematic effort has been made to inventory the genre since Ulrich Conrads's classic *Programs and Manifestoes on 20th-Century Architecture (Programme und Manifeste zur Architektur des 20. Jahrhunderts)*, now already fifty years old.[2] (1) Conrads's book was a rejoinder to manifestos that were in the air in the late 1950s. Appalled by what he saw as the "crass subjectivity" and "anarchical caprice" of Friedensreich Hundertwasser's 1958 *Verschimmelungsmanifest gegen den rationalismus in der architektur (Mould Manifesto against Rationalism in Architecture)* Conrads mounted a counter-attack to Hundertwasser's assault on functionalist modernism.[3] (2) Confidently slim, matter-of-fact, and prefaced by less than 300 words, Conrads's

1 Cover of *Programme und Manifeste zur Architektur des 20. Jahrhunderts* by Ulrich Conrads (1981, originally published in 1964).

collection had no doubt what a manifesto was, nor which ones mattered. When Charles Jencks and Karl Kropf compiled *Theories and Manifestoes of Contemporary Architecture* roughly thirty years later, the opening salvo was aimed at Conrads's book, which had helped, they argued, to "turn the architectural manifesto into predictable event."[4] Jencks sought to detach the manifesto from the avant-garde legacy, seeing it as a broader, more perennial and changeable form, marked by the tension between violent flights of rhetorical passion on the one hand, and a deep-seated, Old Testament propensity for handing down laws, on the other.[5] Despite the desire for greater inclusiveness and a mania for categorization, the book actually contains very few texts that are explicit manifestos.[6] As a result, the vast majority of the manifestos produced during the last fifty years remain scattered in archives, like so much unexploded ordinance waiting to be unearthed. The contributions collected here might be considered an initial set of probes into such territory. They are the fruit of two daylong meetings, the first at Columbia University's Graduate School of Architecture, Planning and Preservation, and the second at the Architecture Faculty of the University of Navarra in 2012, that brought together architects, scholars, and editors to consider the enduring rhetorical traits, printed forms, and modes of action of the genre.

2 Hundertwasser, Demonstration Against Rationalism in Architecture, Vienna (1968).

Literary theorists have turned considerable attention to the form's rhetorical conventions.[7] A manifesto is typically a text defined by conviction, urgency, and immediacy, seeking to push the domain of words as close as possible to the domain of deeds. The force and persuasion of manifestos appear frequently in the proliferation of injunctions, formulated with modal verbs—must, can, shall, will. The temperature of such injunctions can be modulated considerably, ranging from the imperative to the subjunctive, from command and demand to a more nuanced play between desired and hypothetical states of affairs, between possibility and doubt. Such injunctions often appear in the guise of theses or numbered points; condensing thought with emphatic precision, they concentrate the effort of the text. If they are often full of points, manifestos are also fond of pointers, those pronouns indicating the place and time of utterance, as well as the objects of concern: "here," "now," "today," "this." Such pointers direct the reader toward something outside the text; indeed, the manifesto operates as a special kind of text, drawing the reader's attention to the page in order to direct it immediately back out toward the world. As significant as the pointers are the shifters: personal pronouns like "I," "you," and especially "we." The play of such pronouns has a particularly important function in manifestos. "We" remains a tricky type of plural expression; its exact referent often remains ambiguous, capable of referring to a defined group, but also to a larger, unspecified collectivity the reader is invited to join. "We" can mobilize a powerful provisional constituency, proposing forms of solidarity that can allow an individual to appear to be many, yet it is also a pronoun that can disable disagreement and run roughshod over differences.

The earliest texts to bear the name "manifesto" appear in the sixteenth century and are closely allied with power—printed declarations by princes and kings that manifested the sovereign's power to make decisions about war, defense, and other matters of consequence. Early religious tracts also left an enduring stamp on the form, the most famous being the ninety-five theses of Martin Luther's 1517 *Disputatio pro declaratione virtutis indulgentiarum*, which recodified elements from traditions of scholarly debate and religious revelation into a new type of militant document. Karl Marx and Friedrich Engels's 1848 *Communist Manifesto* effected the transformation of the modern manifesto into a tool of political struggle, consolidating and recasting the form in ways that later political and artistic manifestos would continue to echo and rework. The modern genre of the manifesto could thus be seen to occupy and take hold of a particular rupture in authority, one associated both with the breakdown of royal control over the reproduction of the printed word and royal entitlement to the form itself. The royal manifesto was a document that confirmed word as deed, publicly displaying the power of the sovereign's declaration. The rise of the modern political and revolutionary manifesto in the nineteenth century reverses these dynamics, such that the manifesto becomes a form for challenging rather than confirming the legitimacy of a particular authority. As Martin Puchner has insightfully argued, revolutionary manifestos like that of Marx and Engels can be seen as speech acts that lacked the authority to sanction their words as deed, and thus necessarily projected this union into a revolutionary future.[8] On the one hand such projection called forth of a subject, party, group, or class, which would emerge to realize the authority of the manifesto. Yet such a notion could also help to think about the performativity of much of the twentieth-century's manifesto architecture. From Antonio Sant'Elia's drawings of Futurist transport stations in 1914 to Ludwig Mies van der Rohe's 1921 Glass Skyscraper photomontages, and beyond, manifesto projects are projects cast toward the future, figures that the architectural imagination will chase for years before they will be realized in built form.

If the projective capacities of the manifesto are undoubtedly powerful, to read manifestos only as declarations of polemical confidence and law-like clarity would be to miss their often intimate connection to uncertainty, to overlook those moments in which they point us to sources of doubt and objects of concern. Manifestos, after all, have flourished in times of trouble; in the lead-up to World War I and in its aftermath, amid the rubble after World War II, and again from the early 1960s to the mid-1970s, a period marked by the wars of decolonization and Vietnam, the rise of terrorism, and environmental and energy crises. In this sense, the manifesto remains a more ambivalent genre that one might expect. As Puchner reminds us, on the one hand, the writer of the manifesto could never summon the courage to seize the authority that he or she does not yet possess without a type of theatrical confidence. At the same time, such claims are haunted by their own theatricality, afraid that the necessary illusions sustaining a belief in the forward thrust of modernity will turn out to be an empty promise.[9] As the manifesto is relayed more intensely in our own time, we might ask what new performative figures will it call onto the scene? By the same token, we might ask, what types of authority, existing or yet to be realized, are being appealed to?

One source of the manifesto's renewed appeal may be a recognition of the important role it has played in making claims upon the discipline. The contributions compiled here highlight a wide spectrum of such claims, to which can be added a selection of examples drawn from manifestos that have, to greater or lesser extent, marked the course of architectural culture over the last half-century. While by no means exhaustive or exclusive, these brief examples can be grouped into four broad types of recurring claims: claims upon history, claims upon hierarchies within the field, claims on forms of collective identity, and claims on the very media that circulate manifestos.

For a genre so often associated with the future, manifestos frequently ground their claims in attacks on prevailing ideas about history, provoking by means of condensed, biased, and often extreme forms of historical revision. The opening line of Antonio Sant'Elia and Filippo Tommaso Marinetti's *1914 "Futurist Architecture (L'architettura Futurista)"* set a high bar: "Since the Eighteenth century there has been no more architecture."[10] (3) While few postwar manifestos tempt a similar level of bombast, they too stake their claims upon historical revision. Asger Jorn's 1954 exchange with Max Bill over the newly founded Hochschule für Gestaltung at Ulm called for an "artistic revolution to confront the dead language of cubism and constructivism."[11] (4) Jorn aimed to destroy what he saw as an academic recuperation of prewar avant-gardes, even as he sought to claim aspects of this legacy for his own purposes. While coming from a entirely different perspective, *Archigram* magazine's first editorial in 1961 invoked a similar sentiment, vowing to "bypass the decaying Bauhaus image…

3 Antonio Sant'Elia, *Manifesto of Futurist Architecture* (1914).

4 Cover of *Pour la forme* by Asger Jorn (1958).

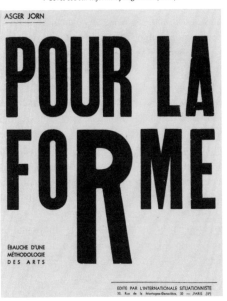

5 Peter Cook and David Greene, cover of *Archigram* 1 (1961).

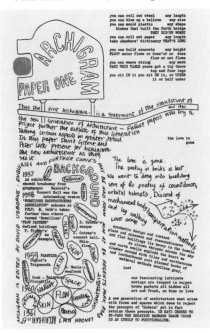

an insult to functionalism."[12] (5) In both cases, to remain true to a revolutionary history meant turning against its contemporary legacy. Still others invoked historical rupture related not to the legacy of the avant-garde, but to technological change. As the sixties drew to a close in Japan, Kisho Kurokawa's "Capsule Declaration" (1969) announced the arrival of Cyborg architecture: "Almost all devices which have been introduced into human society since the Industrial Revolution perform the role of a tool.... Cyborg architecture, on the other hand, is an object in itself. The human being in the capsule and the film which protects his life constitute a new existence."[13] (6) As José Manuel Pozo reminds us, not all postwar manifestos spoke the language of rupture; the form was equally taken up to advance more conservative agendas. In Spain under General Franco's dictatorship, the *Manifiesto de la Alhambra* (1953) reinterpreted this monument as an

6 The works of Kisho Kurokawa, poster by Kiyoshi Awazu (1970).

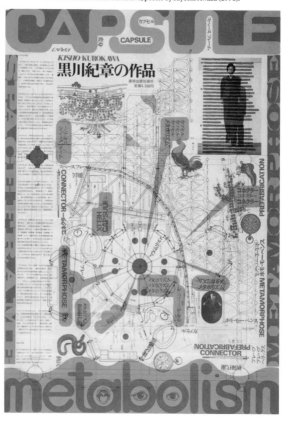

urgent and timely manifesto for contemporary Spanish architecture at the very moment that the country was beginning to reopen to the winds of international culture. And as Enrique Walker argues, in the aftermath of the tumultuous decade of the 1960s the manifesto was not rejected outright, but rather its relationship to history underwent a radical reversal, most emblematically in what Rem Koolhaas has dubbed the "retroactive manifesto." Whereas manifestos typically announce an agenda in advance of any evidence that might sustain their claims, the retroactive genre proceeds by deducing a manifesto from assembled historical evidence. Walker's assessment of the current situation remains pessimistic; if the genre of the retroactive manifesto has increasingly become a cliché, and the classic manifesto has been subjected to a revival, both forms have largely absconded from their original task: advancing arguments within the field.

Alongside such polemical claims on history, manifestos have also taken aim at reigning hierarchies, provoking doubt about the ways in which the field separates the central from the marginal, and the consequential from the trivial. The brief, eight-point "Doorn Manifesto" (1954)—by a group of young architects who would form the kernel of Team Ten—begins with a strident embrace of the larger complexities of human association and community: "It is useless to consider the house except as a part of a community owing to the interaction of these on each other."[14] (7) The effort

7 Team Ten, typescript of "Habitat," also known as the "Doorn Manifesto" (1954).

to reconceptualize community seized on a term that had been left out of the hierarchy of urban functions defined by the 1933 Athens Charter, and was calculated as the opening salvo in an effort to decisively reform the Congrès Internationale d'Architecture Moderne (CIAM). As Anthony Vidler boldly suggests, while the "Doorn Manifesto" aimed to mark a new beginning, it may actually mark the closing of a cycle—the last of the modern genre. In architecture, he argues, not only are such manifestos more rare than we care to believe, since the mid-1950s the cultural politics of the field have steadily gravitated away from such manifesto statements and toward forms of discourse more closely associated with the tradition of the treatise. The 1960s, however, did see a wide range of different claims that sought to challenge the limits of the discipline, perhaps none as maximal as Hans Hollein's 1968 manifesto "Alles ist Architektur" ("Everything is Architecture"). (8) When everything from pills to television broadcasts, and from pyramids to space capsules can be understood as architecture, disciplinary boundaries become nearly impossible to draw. Here a polemical questioning of cultural hierarchy was aligned with a shift in architectural attitude, from a strict concentration on buildings to an experimental appraisal of the architectural implications of diverse types of objects, media, and technological systems. Felicity Scott turns our attention to the

8 Cover of "Alles ist Architektur" by Hans Hollein (1968).

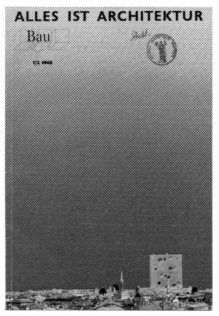

AFTER THE MANIFESTO

1970s and early 1980s, drawing on three very different documents that remain outside of existing anthologies—the Morningstar Commune's "Open Land" manifesto (1970), Leslie Kanes Weisman's "Women's Environmental Rights: A Manifesto" (1981), and Luc Deleu's "Orban Planning Manifesto" (1980). (9) In each case, she highlights how environmental concerns not normally seen as central to the discipline—from building regulations to gender norms and communications media— were mobilized tactically by these manifestos in order to highlight, challenge, and temporarily evade forms of control embedded in architecture's more mundane juridical codes and institutional procedures. It was also during the second half of the 1970s that Bernard Tschumi reappropriated the manifesto form at the very moment when it seemed to be falling out of favor. As he reminds us here, his series of architectural manifestos exhibited in New York and London were crucial early links in a project he has pursued ever since: the identification of architecture with the making of concepts, rather than forms, contexts, or materials. In these manifestos Tschumi went beyond the marginal to stake a claim on the repressed and the taboo. Calling attention to perversity, transgression, and excess was a bid to reveal, and thus open to question, the ever-shifting dynamics around the definition of rules in architecture, together with the moral economies subtending such definitions.

9 Cover of *Heresies* 11, "Making Room: Women and Architecture" (1981), which contained Leslie Kanes Weisman's "Women's Environmental Rights: A Manifesto."

If manifestos have been a platform for challenging established hierarchies of knowledge, they have also served to support the formation of new identities. As Mark Wigley suggests, the "we" in a manifesto is less the designation of the group authoring the statement than a pact of complicity the author seeks with the reader. The condition of possibility for the formation of such new groups often depends on how compellingly a manifesto constructs the image of an older group or existing situation. The "real art" of the manifesto, he continues, lies less in commotion or uproar than in "making it seem that the world is still—waiting for the manifesto." Some of the starkest examples can be found in the militant documents that issued from the occupations and strikes of architectural students in the years around 1968. (10) Consider, for instance, the open letter to André Malraux issued by the occupiers of the Order of French Architects, which demanded "...the abrogation of the Order of French Architects' law of foundation, dictated by the Vichy government in 1940. Our new structures are being elaborated at the heart of the new autonomous and critical university, through the permanent confrontation between workers, students, architect-teachers, and user's associations."[15] Calling into question the legitimacy of the existing, official body of the profession—whose origins were a legacy of France's collaborationist Vichy government—the statement quickly shifts from present to future, uniting the disparate range of identities within the "we"—workers, students, teachers, user groups—in the task of building a new, autonomous, self-managed university. By no means, however, were all affirmations of such shared identities as explicitly oppositional. The postwar years also saw new forms of identification attuned to the period's fascination with biology and cybernetics, particularly as metaphors

10 Cover of *Le carré bleu* no. 3/4, (1968) Special issue dedicated to May 1968.

for processes of continuous change, feedback, and growth. In Noboru Kawazoe's introduction to the "Metabolist Manifesto" (1960), biological processes of change were offered as a model for a renewal of architectural form, but also for a more flexible type of group identity: "The reason we use such a biological word, *metabolism*, is that we believe design and technology should be a designation of human vitality... In the future, more will come to join 'Metabolism' and some will go: that ensures a metabolic process will also take place in its membership."[16] (11) As Carlos Labarta and Jorge Tárrago point out, the postwar breakup of official bodies formed at an earlier moment of modernity, such as CIAM, allowed for a changed attitude to manifestos. Official charters and collective declarations gave way to groups linked by a more informal exchange of individual statements, as can be seen in the correspondence organized in Jaap Bakema's "Post Box for Habitat Development." (12) It remains a historical irony that perhaps the most widely read manifesto to emerge from postwar Spain—José Antonio

11 Page spreads from *Metabolism: Proposals for a New Urbanism* (1960). Known as the "Metabolist Manifesto."

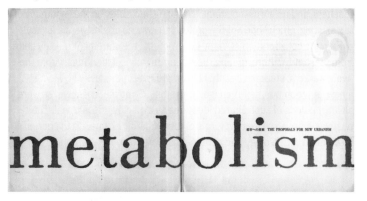

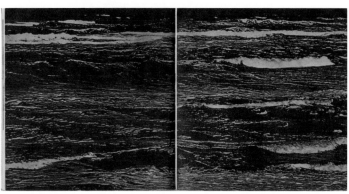

Coderch's "It Is Not Geniuses We Need Now" (1961)—began as a letter circulated through this epistolary network, only acquiring the status of a manifesto through subsequent publication, reprintings, and copies.

Such an example draws attention to the important role of mechanical reproduction; indeed, the history of the manifesto is inextricable from efforts to create new spaces of operation by means of changing media forms. Rubén Alcolea and Héctor García-Diego trace the growing role of photographic reproductions in print media during the 1920s, which was of central importance to architectural manifestos. Proposing the category of the "photo-manifesto" to cover a range of seminal publications by figures such as Le Corbusier, Erich Mendelsohn, and El Lisstizky, they highlight how the process of collecting, organizing, and captioning photographic images overtakes the older linguistic conventions of the genre. As Beatriz Colomina reminds us, the manifesto cannot be separated from the little magazines, journals, and newspapers in which they were published, nor from the role such documents played in creating the very identities of many architects and avant-garde groups. Even a figure like Ludwig Mies van der Rohe, who is often thought of as an architect of few words, completely transforms himself in the early 1920s by forging a link between manifesto texts and manifesto projects, radically redefining the course of his work, and of modern architecture, in ways that continue to be revisited and rewritten. Citing SANAA's 2008 project for Mies's Barcelona Pavilion, she proposes the emergence of a new genre—the soft manifesto—an endgame to the long sequence of buildings, journals, and texts through which the twentieth century's manifesto architecture evolved. Such an endgame can also be seen as a moment of transition. As communications media in our own day continue to transform our sense of space and time in ways as drastic as those of the 1920s or the 1960s, what changed forms might the

12 Letters exchanged in Jaap Bakema's "Post Box for Habitat Development."

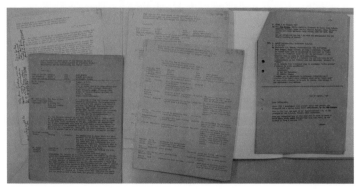

manifesto inhabit, and what new experiences might it claim for architectural thinking?

The question returns us to the initial impetus for this collection—what does the longer history of the manifesto enable one to think as it undergoes its present resurgence? From the mid-nineteenth century onward, the manifesto emerged as a mode for capturing attention amid the growing flood of documents and information unleashed by mass print culture. If it took its impetus from the urgencies of the day, the manifesto also took its measure from the most immediate, cheap, and ephemeral media available—the pamphlet, the newspaper, the little magazine, the broadsheet, the poster—media that could reduce the amount of time separating the creation of a message from its transmission to a mass public. Its visual cues have been drawn more often from the world of advertising and mass communication than from the book. The book, Alphonse de Lamartine pointed out as early as 1830, was already too slow to keep up with the rapid changes of the nineteenth century; the future of writing lay with the newspaper.[17] When Marshall McLuhan repeated Lamartine's words, some 120 years later, newspapers and magazines had long secured their dominance, and were in turn becoming acutely aware of competition from the more instantaneous media of radio and television.[18] In our own time, the gap between writer and public has been compressed even more radically. And while none are the same, all of these media forms continue to exist, however tenuously, today. Once separate media are undergoing a massive convergence and recombination through online forms of distribution, channeling a vastly expanded stream of changeable information, filtered by interfaces that appear and disappear, mutate and reconfigure at a rate only slightly slower than the things they convey. The modern genre of the manifesto crystallized within this same historical horizon, and it, too, remains with us—its history a set of landmarks on the battleground for attention. This struggle for attention may have a special meaning for architects, whose intellectual work must operate across a remarkably broad spectrum of time, from the extremely fast to the agonizingly slow. In an era that prizes instantaneity, the materialization of buildings remains a time-consuming affair. Architectural thinking is stretched between the actuality of the present—the temporality of drawing and writing, of journals and books, of emails and faxes, of blogs and tweets—and the schedules of builders, the production times of manufacturers, the deliberations of competitions and commissions, the credit lines of clients, and the crises and cycles of the broader economy. Paradoxically, might the most urgent message of past manifestos today be not to move faster, but rather to claim more time in a period when it seems in ever-shorter supply? Not to think quicker, but to think longer and harder? Architectural thought, subject as it is to immediate demands and incessant delays, may be in a unique position to reexamine the dynamics of attention in our present era. If the manifesto has long sought to capture and communicate the urgency of the actual, it is also one of those few forms that can be traced across the longer history of architectural modernity. In this, it might even be seen as a special type of relay, one that transmits such urgent signals forward in time, but which also encapsulates the past's claims on the future, in words and forms that aim to be the barometer against which some future present will take its measure.

1   The number of events in recent years themed as, or devoted to, manifestos is too numerous to inventory. One the earliest events to mark this resurgence was the *Manifesto Marathon* organized in the Frank Gehry-designed Serpentine Pavilion in 2008. In 2009, the Manifesto project (http://www.manifestoproject.it/) began gathering and exhibiting design manifestos in galleries around the Europe. In 2010, New York's Storefront for Art and Architecture initiated its manifesto series, an ongoing set of events devoted to the articulation of new positions in the field. In 2009, the Architectural Association, London, advertised an event in which each presented manifesto (of not more than one minute) was rewarded with a free beer. As I write this text, the upcoming 2014 Istanbul Design Biennial has invited participants from around the world to submit manifestos, asking how the manifesto can be "reclaimed for the 21st century."

2   Ulrich Conrads, ed. *Programme und Manifeste zur Architectur des 20. Jahrhunders* (Berlin: Ullstein, 1964). Published in England as *Programmes and Manifestoes on 20th-Century Architecture,* trans. Michael Bullock (London: Lund Humphries, 1970), and subsequently in the United States as *Programs and Manifestoes on 20th-Century Architecture,* (Cambridge, MA: MIT Press, 1971).

3   Ibid.

4   Charles Jencks and Karl Kropf, *Theories and Manifestoes of Contemporary Architecture* (London: Wiley and Sons, 2005 [1997]).

5   See Charles Jencks, "The Volcano and the Tablet," in Jencks and Kropf, *Theories and Manifestoes of Contemporary Architecture*, 2.

6   As Anthony Vidler points out in this volume, there is only one text in the book that explicitly announces itself as a manifesto. Composed almost solely from excerpts from longer works, Jencks and Kropf's compendium may be seen as a testament to a masterful form of manifesto editing, one that expertly extracts the most prescriptive moments from much longer, more analytical, and more nuanced, articles, books, and catalogues.

7   For an early overview, see for instance, *Littérature* (special issue on *Les manifestes*), October 1980. More recently, a number of volumes have engaged the subject. See Janet Lyon, *Manifestos: Provocations of the Modern* (Ithaca, NY: Cornell University Press, 1999); Mary Ann Caws, "The Poetics of the Manifesto," in *Manifesto: A Century of Isms* (Lincoln, NE: University of Nebraska Press, 2001), xix-xxxi; Luca Somigli, *Legitimizing the Artist: Manifesto Writing and European Modernism* (Toronto: University of Toronto, 2003); Nicola Lees, ed., *Serpentine Gallery Manifesto Marathon,* (London: Koenig, 2009); and Alex Danchev, ed., *100*

Artists' Manifestos: From the Futurists to the Stuckists (London: Penguin Books, 2011).

8   Martin Puchner, *Poetry of the Revolution: Marx, Manifestos, and the Avant-Gardes* (Princeton, NJ: Princeton University Press, 2006).

9   Ibid., 26.

10   Antonio Sant'Elia and Filippo Tommaso Marinetti, "Futurist Architecture" (1914), in Conrads, *Programs and Manifestoes on 20th-Century Architecture*, 34–38.

11   Asger Jorn, "Arguments apropos of the International Movement for an Imaginist Bauhaus, against an Imaginary Bauhaus, and Its Purpose Today" (1957). Originally published in *Pour La Forme, ébauche d'une méthodologie des arts* (Paris: Editions Internationale Situationniste, 1958), trans. in Joan Ockman, ed., *Architecture Culture 1943–1968* (New York: Rizzoli International Publications, 1993), 172–75.

12   *Archigram 1* (1961), reprinted in Peter Cook, ed., *Archigram* (London: Studio Vista, 1972).

13   Kisho Kurokawa, "Capsule Declaration," trans. in *Metabolism in Architecture* (London: Studio Vista, 1977), 75–82.

14   "The Doorn Manifesto" (1954), in *Team 10 Primer* (Cambridge, MA: The MIT Press, 1968), 75.

15   Occupiers of the Order of French Architects, "Lettre ouverte adressé au ministre des affaires culturelles" (May 22, 1968), *Le Carré Bleu* 3/4 (1968), n.p.

16   Kiyonori Kikutake, Noboru Kawazoe, Noriaki Kurokawa, Masato Ohtaka, and Fumihiko Maki, *Metabolism 1960: Proposals for a New Urbanism* (Tokyo: Bijutsu Shuppan-Sha, 1960), 4.

17   Alphonse de Lamartine, "Sur la Politique Rationelle," *Oeuvres de Lamartine* (Brussels, 1840), 744.

18   Marshall McLuhan, *Counterblast* (Toronto, 1954), n.p., reprinted in *Counterblast* (Berkeley, CA: Gingko Press, 2011).

FROM MANIFESTO TO DISCOURSE

ANTHONY VIDLER

LET ME BEGIN with a modest inquiry into the etymology of the word "manifesto." "Manifest" comes from the Old French word *manifeste*, which in turn comes from the Latin *manifestus*, meaning "struck by the hand, palpable, evident, made clear." *Manifestus* itself comes from the conjoining of two words: *manus*, or "hand," and *festus*, "struck"—which itself derives from *infestare*, "to attack" or "to trouble," and is closely related to *infestus*, "to be hostile, to be bold, attack, to overrun in large numbers, to be harmful or bothersome, to swarm over, to be parasitic in or on a host." Countering this set of negatives, the Latin *festum* also means "feast," or "celebration." In short, this means that at the same time as manifestos make trouble they also celebrate the fact.

It is well established that the first modern manifesto—indeed the first of its kind to form the modern form of the manifesto in its most complete guise—was *Manifest der Kommunismtischen Partei,* written by Karl Marx and Friedrich Engels in 1847 and published the next year (1). What they

1 Karl Marx and Friedrich Engels, *Manifest der Kommunistischen Partei* (1848).

invented was an entire genre, brilliantly concocted from a wide range of previous genres and eloquently rolled into a single form that continued to operate not only in politics but also in poetics for more than a century. Nevertheless, it is a form that, despite attempts to revive it from time to time, has for all intents and purposes now fallen into disuse, or rather, has seemed to outlive its use.

Now this is a contentious statement, especially for those artistic, architectural, poetic, and literary movements that have couched their post-World War II statements of principle in the form of manifestos, but it will, I hope, become clear that I define "use" not in terms of intention—that of the writer—but in terms of context—that of the audience. And I would hold that from the high times of manifesto writing—i.e., from 1848, through 1945—there has been a significant shift in the forms through which any cultural revolution is parsed, and a corresponding shift against the manifesto as the defining genre of the trade.

Let me return for a moment to the genre itself as cooked up by Marx and Engels. Where did this astoundingly influential model come from? How did this text—one that Martin Puchner in his brilliant study *Poetry of the Revolution: Marx, Manifestos, and the Avant-Gardes* counted as influencing "the course of history more directly and lastingly that almost any other text" —come into being, so to speak, seemingly out of whole cloth and ready to be adopted, as it was from 1909 on, as a genre equally effective in cultural realms as in political arenas? "The answer to this question," Puchner writes, "must be sought not so much in the history of revolutions but in the Manifesto itself, and must be sought not only in its content but also in its form."[1]

As a form it was indeed a strange hybrid: for traditionally what was called a manifest was not at all revolutionary, but rather a dictate—the declaration of the will of a sovereign, a state, or its military. But it was also connected to a potentially more subversive act, the religious act of revelation, or, manifestation—the tradition of the apocalyptic revelations of Saint John—and this link to the apocalypse was folded into the Marxian genre, too. Thus the manifesto becomes both a call to action (military or otherwise) and a revelation (religious or otherwise). Historically, this amalgam was first adopted by Luther on behalf of the Reformation (the Ninety-five Theses), and then used against him by Thomas Müntzer for the Swabian peasant revolt, and by the Diggers and Gerrard Winstanley in their radical revolt against the Puritan Revolution in England (2). In each case the tracts of the more violent revolutionaries were couched in apocalyptic formulations. Indeed the radical Puritans, the Levellers, were the first to call their statement a "manifesto" (1649)—coincidentally exactly two centuries before Marx and Engels—thence to be inscribed in the history of radical revolutions traced by Marx himself (3). If we add to this the fundamental Declaration of Independence, and the French Revolutionary Declaration of the Rights of Man, the genre is ready to be completed (4). But with one significant difference.

The "manifestos" that preceded Marx's were all founded within a sense that history formed a continuity out of which would be born reform or revolution. For Marx and Engels, however, as described in their correspondence, the aim was to rewrite history itself, reframe it entirely, so as to conceive it as a continuous process of evolving revolution, toward a new and imminent revolution—"history-as-revolution," as Puchner has noted.[2] *The Communist Manifesto* was something more however; it was a special kind of what J. L. Austin would call a speech act—the transformation of words into actions. As Puchner has it, Marx and Engels achieved the performative content of their manifesto by combining a sense of total authority

2 Martin Luther, the Ninety-Five Theses (1517).

drawn from history, a challenge to the present to recognize this history, as a brilliantly theatrical gesture, and a clear position from which, they, as authors channeling this history, spoke. All these attributes will, as we will see, be taken over by the cultural avant-gardes of the twentieth century.

Thus we get the "haunting" of the "specter of communism," a reference to the ghost of Hamlet's father; or the famous phrase "All that is solid melts into air," echoing the last lines of *The Tempest*. (It is an irony of history, as Puchner points out, that both these phrases come not from the original manifesto, but from the literary traditions of the second translator of the *Manifesto* into English, Samuel Moore. In German the literal translations of these phrases would be more like "a frightful hobgoblin stalks through Europe," or "Everything feudal and fixed evaporates.")[3]

This, however, does not detract from the importance of the position from which the speaker speaks—and the importance for manifestos to possess an oral, theatrical ring to them in order to assert the backing of history, or its entire revision; the deep structure of a quasi-religious credo;

3 John Lilburn, William Walwyn, Thomas Prince, and Richard Overton, Leveller pamphlet, *A Manifestation* (1649).

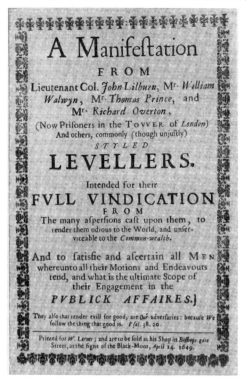

the anticipation of apocalypse in the present; and the assumption of the possibility, if not the immediate inevitability, of a revolution. All make a genre, ready for the picking.

And, we remember, it *was* so picked—by F. T. Marinetti and his friends in Milan as proclaimed in "Le Futurisme" in 1909, on the front page no less, of the French daily newspaper *Le Figaro* (5). Not even Marx was given that spread. The structure of this early foray into the aesthetic manifesto instantly became a classic. First the location was sketched: "We have been up all night my friends and I;" then the back story—in the claustrophobic surroundings of their parents' over-decorated and decadent apartment; then the revolutionary gesture—racing from the past into the future in their new automobiles; then the apocalyptic revelation or rather baptism— immersion in and emerging out of the canal-side mud, as if the writer was new born and sucking on the teats of his Sudanese nurse (a primitive rebirth indeed); and then finally the *credo*: "we believe," "we call," "we deny," "we . . ." etc. etc. The rest is, so to speak, history—the history of a genre,

4 Thomas Jefferson et. al., United States Declaration of Independence (1776).

reformulated, readopted for new purposes, reinterpreted, and rewritten on behalf of artistic and cultural revolution; an effective genre for almost every avant-garde movement in the period 1909 to 1968.

But what about the architectural manifesto? Was this a specific genre of its own, following the respective political and cultural manifestos of Marx and Marinetti? In this context we can see that the architectural manifesto, following Marinetti, was conceived in order to destroy the authority of the *disciplinary treatise*, the preferred form of architectural discourse since the rediscovery of Vitruvius in the Renaissance, the last of which, by Julien Guadet, was published at the very end of the nineteenth century (6, 7). During the following decades it was clear that Marx and Marinetti had had their effect—in the avant-garde manifestos of this period history was suspended in favor of a complete overturning of traditional theory and practice. As Marx had noted in his essay on the failure of the 1848 revolution, "The social revolution of the nineteenth century cannot

5 F.T. Marinetti, "Le Futurisme," in *Le Figaro* (1909).

derive its poetry from the past but only from the future. It cannot begin with itself, before it has shed all superstitious belief in the past… The revolution of the nineteenth century must let the dead bury the dead in order to

6 Vitruvius, index to the *Ten Books on Architecture* (c. 15 BC).

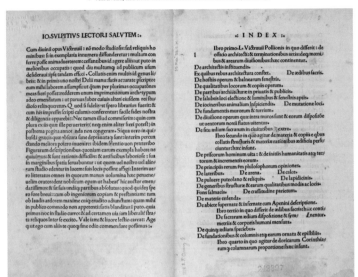

7 Julien Guadet, *Éléments et théorie de l'architecture* (1909 edition).

arrive at its own content. There the phrase exceeded the content. Here the content exceeds the phrase."[4] The architects of the early twentieth century were of the same mind: abstraction and the suspension of history went hand in hand in order to erase all traces—or so it was hoped—of the academic system of classicism and the styles.

Architectural manifestos proper, however, surprisingly did not proliferate as they did in the other arts. Antonio Sant'Elia had to be induced by Marinetti to compose (or be credited with) a manifesto of Futurist architecture in 1914; the De Stijl group published five explicit manifestos; Oskar Schlemmer published a "Manifesto for the First Bauhaus Exhibition" in 1923; the Russians under the influence of and contesting the dictates of Futurism published quite a few—among them Malevich's *Suprematist Manifesto* of 1924 (8). On the whole, architects tended to prefer "theses," "principles," "tenets," "definitions," or "projects," rather than outright manifestos, in an attempt to preserve the essence of what they were purporting to destroy.

8 Antonio Sant'Elia, perspective from *La Città Nuova* (1914).

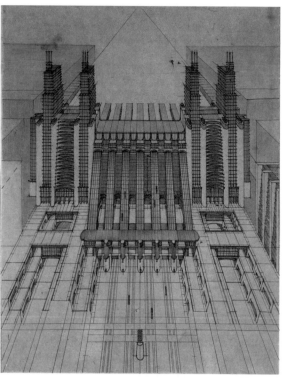

FROM MANIFESTO TO DISCOURSE

Indeed the test came with Le Corbusier, correctly accused by Reyner Banham of hiding his academicism beneath the rhetoric of abstraction and the idea rather than the fact of technological progress. Le Corbusier openly stated his dislike of Futurism in the preface to *Vers une architecture*, and certainly had the intention of writing the next great treatise, but nevertheless interspersed his didactic chapters on working principles for architectural form and function with what one might call residual or analogical manifesto statements italicized at the head of each chapter (9).

In this sense, the title of the first anthology of such statements, Ulrich Conrads's *Programs and Manifestoes on 20th-Century Architecture*, published in German in 1964, was apt enough.[5] In this little volume, which formed the basis for "theory" courses over the next two decades, Conrads published some 60 "programs," from Henry van der Velde's "Programme" of 1903 to Yona Friedman's 1962 "Ten Principles of Space Town Planning," but very few that were truly "manifestos." Here the difference between a program and a manifesto became specific, and the

9 Le Corbusier, *Vers une architecture* (1923).

Centrale électrique de Gennevilliers. Turbine de 40,000 kw.

ARCHITECTURE
OU RÉVOLUTION

reluctance of architects to join with their artist friends was patent, and an intimation of what was to come in the 1960s and '70s, when, despite the revolutionary affect of the era, the manifesto became almost extinct, at least in architecture.

But before becoming extinct, of course, the manifesto had to be historicized. For Conrads's book was the direct heir and result of Banham's research in the late 1950s into the origins and history of the Modern Movement. It was after all Banham who had publicized the Futurist manifestos of Marinetti and Sant'Elia in the *Architectural Review* in the mid-1950s, and his history was in effect a way of relegating the manifesto culture of the first half of the century to its proper, if covert, academic home, all the while trying to associate himself with a new manifesto culture based on technological progressivism; hence his 1955 essay "The New Brutalism," which called for an "architecture autre," and his "Taking Stock" articles of 1960 (10).[6] As a result, it was Conrads's anthology that we read in school in the late 1960s, in tandem with Banham's *Theory and Design in the First Machine Age* of 1960.

If we take a glance at the contents of the next few anthologies of architectural theory statements, the decline of the manifesto becomes clear. Joan Ockman's unsurpassed collection of 1993 abandoned the words "manifesto" and "program" altogether in *Architecture Culture "A Documentary Anthology" 1943–1968*, a collection consisting almost entirely of longer statements or excerpts from essays.[7] Out of over seventy selections, only one retained the title "manifesto" and, indeed, that one might be counted as the last of its modern genre: the *Doorn Manifesto* of

10 Reyner Banham, "The New Brutalism," in the *Architectural Review* (December 1955).

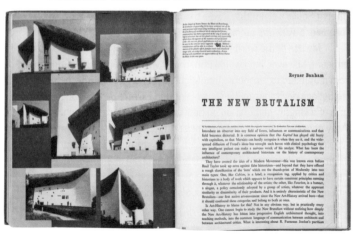

1954, composed by Team Ten's Jaap Bakema, Aldo van Eyck, Blanche van Ginkel, Hans Hovens Greve, Alison and Peter Smithson, and John Voelcker.

Later compilations were even more discursive: Kate Nesbitt's 1996 book, called *Theorizing a New Agenda for Architecture*, was subtitled "An Anthology of Architectural Theory," and contained long selections from even longer books.[8] K. Michael Hays's follow-up collection to Ockman, *Architecture Theory since 1968*, published in 2000, was equally if not more discursive, taking whole long articles and chapters from books.[9] Interpretation, historical examination, analysis, and quasi-philosophical exploration replace the short and sharp manifesto. Revolutionary stridency has given place to a worry about the right way to do architecture not seen since the late nineteenth century.

Indeed, it was a worry that produced not a few attempts to write new treatises for the discipline, a discipline that, threatened by science, technology, and economics, had resorted since the 1960s to a search for (quasi)-autonomy and new guiding principles that would authorize its role in a newly heterogeneous world. Unlike previous treatises, however, these new versions revealed a deep sense of inferiority to adjoining disciplines—to science of course, but also to psychology, and above all to philosophy. Thus Peter Eisenman's claims for the autonomy of formal principles were heavily reliant on the "formal" principles of Gestalt psychology; Christian Norberg-Schultz's *Intentions in Architecture* were derived, despite an apparent neutrality of approach, from his misreading of Heidegger as defining a phenomenological comfort zone rather than the abyssal implications of the author of *Being and Time*.[10] Robert Venturi's *Complexity and Contradiction in Architecture* was more a reflection on modes of interpretation and compositional strategies than a polemic for a new way of designing, despite Vincent Scully's claim that it was the most powerful call to arms since Le Corbusier's *Vers une architecture*.[11]

My use of the word "discursive" in relation to these treatises is not innocent, however. For I would note that it was symptomatic of this shift from manifesto to discourse that Michel Foucault's inaugural lecture at the Collège de France in 1971 was entitled *L'Ordre du discours*, taking the form of a lengthy elaboration on how to conduct "discourse analysis," as a way of unpacking the analysis-resistant "discourses" of the traditionally hegemonic disciplines and ideologies.[12] As interpreted by social and even architectural historians and theorists, this was an open invitation to identify the "discourse" of architecture, which was revealed as not only hegemonic with respect to design ideology but also deeply ramified within a spreading network of relations with other discursive formations, from law to religion to medicine and the like. The brilliance of Foucault's *Surveiller et punir* (*Discipline and Punish*) in selecting Jeremy Bentham and the Panopticon as a trope for the installation of social order for the bourgeois throughout the nineteenth and twentieth centuries relied not so much in its picking on architecture as a tool of such order, but in revealing the complex complicity of architecture in this order—a complicity to be historicized and theorized by Manfredo Tafuri after 1968 (11).[13]

Thus by a strange twist of fate, critical architectural thought that stood for architectural theory in the 1970s and '80s found itself fundamentally *against* architecture, or at least against the very discipline that the new treatises were trying to reinstate and support. Architecture against itself was at once meta-historical and meta-disciplinary, and thus left very little in the way of principles or rules of composition for the students of these years. If there were any manifesto-like statements, from Guy Debord to Hundertwasser, to R. Buckminster Fuller, to Archizoom or Superstudio, they were statements against architecture—dystopian or techno-Futurist— or, as in the case of Ant Farm, of the innumerable claims for "architecture without architects," proposing simple "returns" to a supposed prelapsarian state of preindustrial, or vernacular self-building.

Today we have inherited all these heterogeneous texts, and despite Charles Jencks's brave attempt to call his own anthology of 2006 *Theories*

11 Jeremy Bentham, plan and section of the Panopticon (1791).

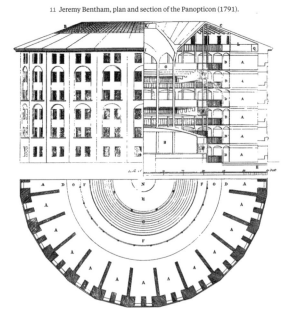

and Manifestos of Contemporary Architecture, only a single manifesto
can be found among his 144 excerpts, and that, a brave one, by Lebbeus
Woods, excerpted from his 1993 *War and Architecture* pamphlet and
written in the true spirit of Futurism (12). I conclude with its echoing tones
that reverberate back through the twentieth century to 1909, but even
more to 1847, and forward to the war-torn present:

> Architecture and war are not incompatible.
> Architecture is war. War is architecture.
> I am at war with my time, with history, with all authority
> that resides in fixed and frightened forms.
> I am one of millions who do not fit in, who have no home, no family,
> no doctrine, nor firm place to call my own, no known beginning or end,
> no "sacred and primordial site."
> I declare war on all icons and finalities, on all histories
> that would chain me with my own falseness, my own pitiful fears.
> I know only moments, and lifetimes that are as moments,

12 Lebbeus Woods, cover of *War and Architecture* (1993).

and forms that appear with infinite strength, then "melt into air."
I am an architect, a constructor of worlds,
a sensualist who worships the flesh, the melody,
a silhouette against the darkening sky.
I cannot know your name. Nor can you know mine.
Tomorrow we begin together the construction of a city.[14]

Woods's cri de coeur might be dismissed now as a romantic nostalgia for a time when such fighting words had real social and architectural resonance—Jencks sandwiches it among a heterogeneous group of dissimilar writings that he dubs "New Modern"—but it does prove that the manifesto form might well have a new life, if only to counter the message of certain contemporary treatises, dedicated as they are to absorbing architecture seamlessly into the technological world of global development.

1   Martin Puchner, *Poetry of the Revolution: Marx, Manifestos, and the Avant-Gardes* (Princeton: Princeton University Press, 2006), 11.

2   Ibid., 23.

3   Ibid., 53.

4   Karl Marx, *The Eighteenth Brumaire of Louis Bonaparte*, in Karl Marx and Friedrich Engels, *Werke*, vol. 8 (Berlin: Dietz Verlag, 1960), 117. Cited in Puchner, *Poetry of the Revolution*, 1.

5   Ulrich Conrads, ed., *Programs and Manifestoes on 20th-Century Architecture* (Cambridge: MIT Press, 1970).

6   See Reyner Banham, "The New Brutalism," *Architectural Review* 118, no. 708 (December 1955), 361; "Futurism and Modern Architecture," *Journal of the Royal Institute of British Architects* 64, no.4 (February 1957), 133; and *Theory and Design in the First Machine Age* (London: The Architectural Press, 1960), where he devotes an entire section to Futurist manifestos and projects.

7   Joan Ockman, ed., *Architecture Culture 1943–1968: A Documentary Anthology* (New York: Rizzoli, 1993).

8   Kate Nesbitt, ed., *Theorizing a New Agenda for Architecture: An Anthology of Architectural Theory 1965–1995* (New York: Princeton Architectural Press, 1996).

9   K. Michael Hays, ed., *Architectural Theory since 1968* (Cambridge: MIT Press, 1998).

10   Christian Norberg-Schultz, *Intentions in Architecture* (Oslo: Universitetsforlaget, 1963).

11   Robert Venturi, *Complexity and Contradiction in Architecture* (New York: The Museum of Modern Art, 1966).

12   Michel Foucault, *L'Ordre du discours* (Paris: Gallimard, 1971).

13   Michel Foucault, *Suveiller et punir* (Paris: Gallimard, 1975); Manfredo Tafuri, "Per una critica dell'ideologia architettonica," *Contropiano* 1 (January-April 1969), trans. Stephen Sartorelli, "Toward a Critique of Architectural Ideology," in Hays ed., *Architectural Theory*, 6-35.

14   Lebbeus Woods, "Manifesto [1993]" in Charles Jencks and Karl Kropf, *Theories and Manifestoes of Contemporary Architecture,* 2nd edition (Chichester: John Wiley, 2006), 304.

MANIFESTO ARCHITECTURE

—

BEATRIZ COLOMINA

1   THE MANIFESTO IS MEDIA. IT DOES NOT EXIST OUTSIDE OTHER MEDIA
       (NEWSPAPER, MAGAZINES, PAMPHLETS, POSTERS, RADIO, ETC.).

2   DESIGN IS PART OF THE ARCHITECTURAL MANIFESTO. IT IS NOT
       JUST THE DESIGN OF THE MANIFESTO, ITS GRAPHICS AND LAYOUT.
       AN ARCHITECTURAL PROJECT CAN BE AN INTEGRAL PART OF
       A MANIFESTO—PART OF THE ARGUMENT, NOT AN ILLUSTRATION.

3   THE MANIFESTO PRECEDES THE WORK. IT IS A BLUEPRINT OF
       THE FUTURE.

4   EVERY MANIFESTO IS A RE-WORKING OF PREVIOUS MANIFESTOS.

5   NEW MEDIA = NEW MANIFESTOS, BUT THEY MAY NO LONGER
       LOOK LIKE MANIFESTOS.

THE HISTORY OF THE AVANT-GARDE (in art, architecture, literature) cannot be separated from the history of its engagement with the media. It isn't just that the avant-garde used media to publicize its work—the work didn't exist before its publication.

Futurism didn't really exist before the publication of the "Le Futurisme" on the front page of *Le Figaro*, the most revered newspaper in Europe, on February 20, 1909. As Caroline Tisdall and Angelo Bozzola have pointed out, "the birth of futurism was a stroke of advertising genius." Even members of the Futurist group (Umberto Boccioni, Carlo Carrà, Giacomo Balla, Gino Severini, Luigi Russolo, and others) were recruited from the manifesto.[1]

Adolf Loos didn't exist before his polemical writings in the pages of newspapers and in his own little magazine *Das Andere*, of which only two issues were published in 1903 (1). As Reyner Banham hinted, when Loos arrived in Paris he was already famous, but his fame was due to his writings—some of which had been translated into French—rather than to his buildings, "which seem to have been known only by hearsay."[2] Loos didn't arrive in Paris until 1922, but he was still known only through his writings, which go back to turn-of-the-century Vienna, and operated like radical manifestos (think *Ornament und Verbrechen* and *Architektur*). Herwarth Walden had published five articles by Loos in his magazine *Der Sturm* by 1912. To have access to the pages of *Der Sturm*, as Banham noted, was to have access to a limited but international audience. It was through this channel that Loos's words arrived in Paris, where his writings were reprinted in other magazines and where he was appreciated by the Dadaists.[3] Loos's only building in Paris was the house for Tristan Tzara in Montmartre (1925-26). Manifesto, once again, preceded building.

Likewise, Le Corbusier didn't exist before his magazine *L'Esprit nouveau* (1920-25) and the books that came out of its polemical pages (*Vers une architecture, Urbanisme, L'art décoratif d'aujourd'hui, Almanach d'architecture moderne*) (2). In fact, the very name Le Corbusier was a pseudonym used for writing about architecture in *L'Esprit nouveau*. He became known as an architect and created a clientele for his practice through these pages. In that sense it can be argued that Le Corbusier was an effect of a set of manifestos.

Even an architect like Mies van der Rohe, who is primarily thought in terms of craft and tectonics, and not as a writer, didn't really exist without *G: Material zur elementaren Gestaltung* (1923-26), the journal that he was part of, and the many little magazines that he contributed to, from *Frühlicht* to *Merz* (3).

1 Adolf Loos, advertisement for *Das Andere* (1903).

Entire groups from Dada and Surrealism to De Stijl became effects of their manifesto-journals. On the occasion of the 1978 Hayward Gallery exhibition *Dada and Surrealism Reviewed*, Rosalind Krauss wrote: "Witnessing the parade of surrealist magazines—*La Révolution surréaliste, Le surréalism au service de la révolution, Documents, Marie, The International Surrealist Bulletin, VVV, Le Surréalisme, même*, and many others—one becomes convinced that *they* more than anything else are the true objects produced by surrealism."[4] Little magazines, photography plus text, and manifestos are the "true" surrealist productions, rather than paintings or sculptures.

Likewise in the 1960s and '70s. Reyner Banham used to tell a story about a limousine full of Japanese architects that one day stopped in the street where he was living in London and asked directions to the office of Archigram. But Archigram didn't really exist as an architectural group yet. *Archigram* was a just little leaflet practically produced in the kitchen of Peter Cook, who lived across the street from Reyner and Mary Banham. Only much later did the loose group of young architects (Peter Cook, Mike Webb, Dennis Crompton, Ron Herron, Warren Chalk, and David

2 Le Corbusier, covers of *L'Espirit Nouveau* 1-4 (1920).

3 Mies van der Rohe, Friedrichstrasse Skyscraper Project,
on the cover of *G: Materialen zur elementaren Gestaltung* no. 3 (June 1924).

Greene) call themselves Archigram, after their magazine (4). And Archigram comes from architecture and "*tele*gram"—once again, architecture as a communication system.

In fact, during this period there was a full-blown explosion of architectural little magazines, which instigated a radical transformation in architectural culture by generating many manifestos. One can argue that during this period little magazines—more than buildings—were, once again, the site of innovation and debate in architecture. Banham could hardly contain his excitement. In an article entitled "Zoom Wave Hits Architecture," of 1966, he throws away any scholarly restraint to absorb the syncopated rhythms of the new magazines in a kind of Futurist ecstasy:

> Wham! Zoom! Zing! Rave!—and it's not Ready Steady Go, even though it sometimes looks like it. The sound effects are produced by the erupting of underground architectural protest magazines. Architecture, staid queen-mother of the arts, is no longer courted by plush glossies and cool scientific journals alone but is having her skirts blown up and her bodice unzipped by irregular newcomers, which are—typically—rhetorical, with-it moralistic, mis-spelled, improvisatory, anti-smooth, funny-format, cliquey, art-oriented but stoned out of their minds with

4 Warren Chalk, *Archigram* 4 cover (1964).

science-fiction images of an alternative architecture that would be perfectly possible tomorrow if only the Universe (and especially the Law of Gravity) were differently organized.[5]

If manifestos and little magazines drove the historical avant-garde of the 1920s, the 1960s and, '70s witnessed a rebirth and a transformation of these polemical publications. In recent years there has been a huge interest in the experimental architecture of this time—from Archigram, the Metabolists, Ant Farm, Superstudio, and Archizoom to Haus-Rucker-Co, and others, dubbed "Radical Architecture" by Germano Celant in 1972—but the manifestos of that revolution have been, for the most part, neglected.

Banham's article itself can be understood as a kind of manifesto—the historian's manifesto exclaiming and exulting over the arrival of the new kind of publication. Even the opening words of his article: "Wham! Zoom! Zing! Rave!" are a reference to F. T. Marinetti's sound poem "Zang Tumb Tumb" (1912), which echoed the sounds of gunfire and explosives of the Battle of Adrianople in the first Balkan War that Marinetti had witnessed as a reporter (5). War and manifesto are inseparable. In its content, Banham's manifesto could be seen as responding, forty years later, to the call from the editors of *G* to abandon traditional art history in favor of writing manifestos:

5 F.T. Marinetti, "Zang Tumb Tumb: Adrianopoli Ottobre: parole in libertà" (October 1912).

Those of you doing art history, take some advice:
Have your manuscripts pulped!
Write manifestos for us!
Live for the thing that exists today------------to the extent you see it.
Learn to see the thing----------to the extent you want to
and
learn to want the thing.
Art history that is not a serious manifesto for the thing will only warm
us is the central heating.[6]

In this spirit, Banham perfected the technique of the short essay, publishing around one thousand punchy texts. In the meantime, another kind of manifesto emerged in the 1960s and '70s in the form of books: Robert Venturi's *Complexity and Contradiction in Architecture* (1966), a self-declared "gentle manifesto," and Rem Koolhaas's *Delirious New York* (1978), a self-declared "retroactive manifesto." And, to insist again, it is not just that we learn about the work of these architects through these publications. The manifesto precedes the work. And the work is understood as an extension of those polemics.

Manifesto Mies

Mies might be the most unexpected yet remarkable case. His place in architectural history—his role as one of the leaders of the Modern Movement—was established through a series of five projects (none of them actually built, or even buildable—they were not developed at that level) he produced for competitions and publications during the first half of the 1920s. I am referring to the 1921 Friedrichstrasse Skyscraper entry for a competition (exhibited at Berlin City Hall), the Glass Skyscraper of 1922, produced for the *Grosse Berliner Kunstausstellung* (Annual Berlin Art Exhibition), the Reinforced Concrete Office Building of 1923, and the Concrete and Brick Country Houses, presented in the Berlin Art Exhibitions of 1923 and 1924 (6). After Berlin, the projects were shown in a number of venues, including the *Internationale Architekturausstellung* (International Architecture Exhibition) at the Bauhaus in Weimar, curated by Walter Gropius, and the exhibition *Les Architectes du groupe De Stijl* (The Architects of the De Stijl Group) at Léonce Rosenberg's Galerie de L'Effort Moderne in Paris organized by Theo van Doesburg, and published in a long list of avant-garde journals, including *Frühlicht*, *G*, *Merz*, and *L'Architecture vivante*, as well as in many books on modern architecture written during the 1920s.[7]

Mies's first writings were also produced in relation to these projects. His first article, "Hochhäuser" ("Skyscrapers"), was published in the first issue of *Frühlicht* (1922); "Bürohaus" ("Office Building") was published in the first issue of *G* in 1923 alongside the Concrete Office Building; and "Bauen" ("Building"), written with Hans Richter, the editor of *G*, appeared framing the Concrete Country House in the second issue of *G* in 1923. Mies wrote a total of seven articles in these years, contributing significantly to the making of his persona.

Zooming in on these articles, they clearly take the form of manifestos. In "Bürohaus," Mies makes a series of stark declarations in the form of a poem and the image of the project of the Concrete Office Building is given exactly the same space on the page as the poem. They are placed side by side, both sitting on top of the bold label "BÜROHAUS," with a gradually more technical description underneath. Statement and project are inseparable. The project is seen to make a statement and the statement is seen as

6 Mies van der Rohe, Friedrichstrasse Skyscraper Project, Berlin (1921).

a project. The image of the project is not an illustration of the statement; it is part of the statement itself (7).

In *G* number 2, Mies repeats the strategy, again insisting on the equivalence of statement and project, and again dividing the text between a series of manifesto declarations and a more detailed technical description, each signed, with the project between occupying the same amount of space as the text (8).[8]

It was also around 1920 that Mies separated from his wife and children in order to dedicate himself fully to architecture and changed his name, Mies, to Miës van der Rohe, adding his mother's family name (Rohe) to his own with the Dutch preposition "van der." According to Sandra Honey, "things Dutch ran high in Germany at the time." Other critics have suggested that he was hoping it would ring close to "von," with its aristocratic overtones. He even added the umlaut to the "e" of Mies, so that the word would be pronounced in two syllables. "Mies" in German means "awkward, nasty, miserable, poor, seedy, out of sorts, bad or wretched."[9] He clearly did not want any of these attributes associated with his work. His entry into the Friedrichstrasse competition was already made under the new name Miës van der Rohe.

It was these five projects, this "paper architecture," together with the publicity apparatus enveloping them, that first made Mies into a historical figure. The houses that he had built so far, and that he would continue to

7 Mies van der Rohe, "Bürohaus", in *G* no. 1 (1923).

develop during the same years, would have taken him nowhere. While it is true that the Riehl House of 1907 was noted by a critic and published in *Moderne Bauformen* and in *Innen Dekoration*, between the somewhat modest articles covering this house in 1910 and his own article in *Frühlicht* in 1922 presenting the glass skyscraper, nothing else of Mies's work was published. Twelve years of silence! Imagine the trauma.

Could we attribute this silence to the blindness of architectural critics of his time, as some historians seem to imply? Mies's attitude is much clearer. In the mid-1920s he destroyed the drawings of most of his work prior to that time, thereby constructing a very precise "image" of himself, one from which all incoherencies, all faux-pas, were erased.[10] Note the parallelism with Adolf Loos, who destroyed all the documents from his projects when he left Vienna for Paris in 1922, and with Le Corbusier, who excluded all his early houses in La Chaux-de-Fonds from publication in his *Oeuvre complète*. A manifesto requires destruction of history, even destruction of one's own history. Still in 1947, Mies did not allow Philip Johnson to publish most of his early work in the monograph that Johnson was preparing as a catalogue for the first "comprehensive retrospective" exhibition of Mies's work at the Museum of Modern Art (MoMA), and that would constitute the first book on Mies. "Not enough of a statement," Mies is supposed to have said about the drawings of an early house project that Johnson wanted to include.[11] Not enough of a statement? Not enough of a manifesto. Mies

8 Mies van der Rohe, Concrete Country House, in *G* no. 2 (1923).

excluded from the exhibition all his more traditional early work up to 1924, with the exception of the project for the Kröller-Müller Villa (1912–13).

And when thirty years later, on the occasion of the third edition of his book, Johnson was asked in an interview, "How would you do the book today?", he answered: "Most of all I would look into . . . the suddenness with which Mies went from what he had been doing to the glass skyscraper of 1921."[12] A key clue to Mies's sudden change of direction was provided by Sandra Honey when she wrote that the breaking point came when Walter Gropius refused to exhibit Mies's project for the Kröller-Müller Villa in his 1919 *Ausstellung für unbekannte Architekten* (Exhibition for unknown architects).[13] According to Mies, Gropius said: "We can't exhibit it, we are looking for something completely different."[14] The failure of this house, a project that Mies was so attached to as to still include it forty-five years later in the MoMA exhibition, or the trauma of that rejection, stimulated a major change in his work. Excluded from an exhibition dedicated to an emergent sensibility, he started designing directly for exhibitions and in so doing revolutionized his work. The competitions, exhibitions, and publications of the early 1920s did not simply give Mies the opportunity to present his first modern projects. The projects were modern precisely because they were produced for those contexts. The exhibition became the site of his laboratory.

Mies's work is a textbook case of a wider phenomenon. Modern architecture became "modern" not as it is usually understood by using glass, steel, or reinforced concrete, but by engaging with the media: with publications, competitions, exhibitions. The materials of communication were used to rebuild the house. With Mies this is literally the case. What had been a series of rather conservative domestic projects realized for real clients (the Riehl House, the Perls House, the Kröller-Müller Villa, the Werner House, the Urbig House) became, in the context of the Berlin Art Exhibition, of *G*, of *Frühlicht*, and so on, a series of manifestos on modern architecture.

Not only that. In Mies one can see, perhaps as with no other architect of the Modern Movement, a true case of schizophrenia between the projects developed for publications and exhibitions and those developed for clients. Still in the 1920s, at the same time that he was developing his most radical designs, Mies could build such conservative houses as the Villa Eichstaedt in a suburb of Berlin (1921–23) and the Villa Mosler in Potsdam (1924) (9). Can we blame these projects on the conservative taste of Mies's clients? Georg Mosler was a banker and his house is said to reflect his taste. But when in 1924 the art historian and Constructivist artist Walter Dexel, who was very much interested in and supportive of modern architecture,[15] commissioned Mies to do a house for him, Mies blew it (10). He was unable to come up with the modern house his client had desired within the deadline. He gave one excuse after another. The deadline was repeatedly postponed. And in the end Dexel gave the project to another architect. In fact, it was not until 1927 that Mies was able to break with tradition, when he managed to use a steel structure and put up non-load-bearing walls in his apartment building at the Weissenhofsiedlung in Stuttgart (11).

9 Mies van der Rohe, Villa Mosler, Potsdam (1924).

10 Mies van der Rohe, sketch for Walter Dexel House, Jena (1924).

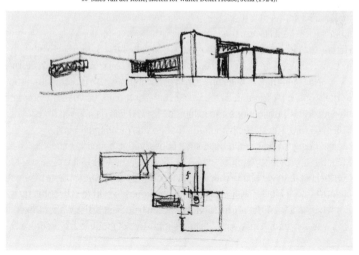

For a long time, then, there was an enormous gap between the flowing architecture of Mies's published projects and his struggle to find the appropriate techniques to produce these effects in built form. For many years he was literally trying to catch up with his publications. Perhaps that is why he worked so hard to perfect a sense of realism in the representation of his projects, as in the photomontage of the Glass Skyscraper with cars flying by on the Friedrichstrasse.

It is not by chance that Mies started to catch up with himself in the context of structures built for exhibitions: his apartment building in the Weissenhofsiedlung in Stuttgart (1927) and the German Pavilion in the 1929 International Exposition in Barcelona. Indeed the most extreme and influential proposals in the history of modern architecture were made in the context of temporary exhibitions. Think about Bruno Taut's Glashaus (the pavilion for the glass industry in the 1914 Werkbund Exhibition in Cologne); Le Corbusier and Pierre Jeanneret's L'Esprit Nouveau Pavilion in Paris (1925); Konstantin Melnikov's USSR Pavilion at the *Exposition internationale des arts décoratifs et industriels moderns* in Paris (1925); Mies and Lilly Reich's "Café Samt und Seide (Velvet and Silk Café)" at the exhibition *Die Mode der Dame*, Berlin (1927), their Glass Room in Stuttgart (1927) and, of course, the Barcelona Pavilion (1929); Alvar Aalto's Finnish Pavilion at the World Exposition, Paris (1937) and his Finnish Pavilion at the 1939 New York World's Fair; Le Corbusier and Iannis Xenakis's Philips Pavilion in Brussels (1958); Buckminster Fuller's Geodesic Dome for the American

11 Mies van der Rohe, apartment building at the Weissenhofsiedlung, Stuttgart (1927).

Exhibition in Moscow (1959) and his U.S. pavilion for Expo '67 in Montreal; Eero Saarinen and Charles and Ray Eames's IBM Pavilion for the 1964 New York World's Fair; Frei Otto's German Pavilion at Expo '67 in Montreal; the Pepsi Pavilion for Expo '70 in Osaka by E.A.T. (Experiments in Art and Technology); Coop Himmelb(l)au's The Cloud, a prototype for future living, designed for Documenta 5 (1972); Aldo Rossi's Il Teatro del Mondo, a temporary theater built for the Venice Architecture Biennale of 1979 to recall the floating theaters of Venice in the eighteenth century, popular during carnivals; and countless other examples. The tradition of the pavilion as the site of architectural experimentation continues into the turn of the century with such mythical projects as Diller + Scofidio's Blur Building in Yverdon-les-Bains, Switzerland, an inhabitable cloud as media pavilion for Swiss Expo 2002 (now destroyed), and the series of pavilions that spring up every year at the Serpentine Gallery in London and include those of Zaha Hadid, Toyo Ito, Oscar Niemeyer, Rem Koolhaas and Cecil Balmond, Frank Gehry, SANAA, Olafur Eliasson and Kjetil Thorsen, and Herzog & de Meuron with Ai Weiwei.

This relentless tradition of exuberant and experimental buildings raises the question of whether the pavilion is itself an architectural manifesto. Architects treat exhibitions, like magazines, as sites for polemical statements about the future. The history of manifestos is inseparable from the history of experimental pavilions. This is a tradition of manifesto through design.

When commissioned to build the German Pavilion for the Barcelona International Exposition in 1929, Mies asked the Ministry of Foreign Affairs what was to be exhibited. That is a normal question for an architect: what is the building for? An artist never needs to ask that. "Nothing will be exhibited," was the answer. "The pavilion itself will be the exhibit."[16] In the absence of a traditional client or program, Mies was able to take his work to new limits and one of the most influential buildings of the century emerged as a pure manifesto.

Mies was treated as an artist in Barcelona. If, according to Gordon Matta-Clark, the difference between architecture and sculpture is that one has plumbing and the other does not, the Barcelona Pavilion is art. The pavilion became an exhibit about exhibition. The only thing it exhibited was a new way of looking.

Manifesto Rewrites

Manifestos always refer to earlier manifestos. Each is a reworking of earlier statements. Mies's polemic in Barcelona, for example, was revisited in the XVII Milan Triennale (1986) when OMA constructed its Casa Palestra

(Body-building home, a Barcelona Pavilion "bent" to fit the curve of its allotted site within the exhibition building):

> By then, phobic about the duty to reveal, we decided to embody our resistance in an exhibit about exhibition. At the time, a clone of Mies's pavilion was being built in Barcelona. How fundamentally did it differ from Disney? In the name of higher authenticity, we researched the true history of the pavilion after the closing of the 1929 International Fair and collected whatever archaeological remnants it had left across Europe on its return journey. Like a Pompeian villa, these fragments were reassembled as far as possible to suggest the former whole, but with one inevitable inaccuracy: since our "site" was curved, the pavilion had to be "bent."[17]

OMA's manifesto echoes and transforms an early manifesto (12). Even the framing of the project echoes Mies's polemical statements in *G* by giving equal value to image and text and signing the text. OMA's manifesto is an homage not only to the Barcelona Pavilion but also to modern architecture, under attack in those years as "lifeless, empty and puritanical": "It has always been our conviction that modern architecture is a hedonistic movement, that its abstraction, rigour and severity are in fact plots to create the most provocative settings for the experiment that is modern life."[18] The earlier manifesto is not just echoed. It is re-launched and rewritten.

12 OMA, Casa Palestra, Milan Triennale (1986).

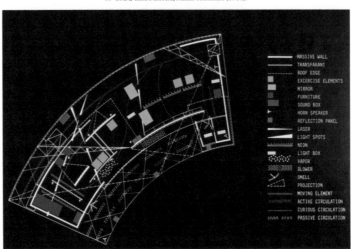

MANIFESTO ARCHITECTURE

In the Casa Palestra the Barcelona Pavilion is inhabited by gymnasts, bodybuilders, and exercise equipment. Mies's minimalist statement becomes engorged with activities. The references multiply. The project alludes to the tradition of the bodybuilding house in modern architecture: from Marcel Breuer's bedroom for Erwin Piscator in Berlin (1927) (13) to Walter Gropius's gym in his apartment for the German Building Exhibition in Berlin (1931), to Richard Döcker's gym on the roof at the Weissenhofsiedlung in Stuttgart (1927), to the 1,000-meter running track that Le Corbusier proposed for the roof of his Immeuble Villas (1922), to Richard Neutra's Lovell House (1929), and even to the transformation in the 1960s of Mies's Tugendhat House in Brno into a children's gym by Communist bureaucrats. OMA takes modern architecture's dream of a healthy body to a new level. Experimentation in exhibitions always becomes collective in the end. Other architects pick up some ideas, work on them, and then are themselves responded to in different exhibitions. That is what architectural discourse is all about—an exchange of manifestos. OMA positions itself here in relationship to its own time, the height of postmodernism and its attack on modern architecture, through a twisting of Mies that unleashes the repressed sensuality of modern architecture. A new manifesto is produced by twisting an old one.

Out-Miesing Mies

The process keeps going. In 2008, SANAA did an installation in the reconstructed Barcelona Pavilion. The project is a classic SANAA move

13 Marcel Breuer, Bedroom for Erwin Piscator, Berlin (1927).

of "out-Miesing" Mies by inserting a transparent curtain into his pavilion. The pavilion is completely transformed by doing almost nothing. As with Mies, Kazuyo Sejima and Ryue Nishizawa are also famous for saying almost nothing. And yet their description of the project is a sophisticated repetition of Mies's manifesto technique. Once again, an image of the design is given equal status to a series of polemical points (14). In a sense, SANAA goes one step forward by having the polemical statements actually spell out the steps in the design process. It is almost like shoptalk that takes us through the process.

This mode of statement itself might be a new kind of subtle manifesto, a soft manifesto, refusing to define the future yet organizing it into a set of points. SANAA's pamphlet is unambiguously a manifesto. It directly echoes the polemical aesthetic of the 1920s posters and pamphlets even as it refuses to play the game:

14, 15 SANAA, Installation in the reconstructed Barcelona Pavilion (2008).

"We decided to use acrylic to make transparent curtains.
We imagined an installation design that leaves the existing space
of the Barcelona Pavilion undisturbed.
The acrylic curtain stands freely on the floor and is shaped in a
calm spiral.
The curtain softly encompasses the spaces within the pavilion and
creates a new atmosphere.
The view through the acrylic will be something different from the
original with soft reflections slightly distorting the pavilion."

SANAA in the Barcelona Pavilion is the ultimate encounter, since SANAA is widely considered the inheritor of Miesian transparency—a "challenge," as Sejima admitted—a return to the scene of the crime, one could argue. The installation carefully marks off a part of the pavilion with an acrylic curtain acting as a kind of crime-scene tape, leaving, as SANAA put it, "the space of the Barcelona Pavilion undisturbed." And yet a completely new atmosphere has been created.

But what crime has been committed here? What has been cordoned off? Is it the freestanding golden onyx wall at the center of the pavilion and the two Barcelona chairs where King Alfonso XIII and Queen Victoria Eugenia of Spain were supposed to sit during the opening ceremonies of the building on May 26, 1929, and sign the golden book? Or is it the space outside the spiral that has been marked off, preserved, "undisturbed"?

In any case, the cordon is loose. The spiral is open. We can walk in, but not so easily. First we have to find the entrance, slide around the outside of the curtain. Only when we are in the other side of the space of the pavilion, having squeezed between the acrylic curtain and the pavilion's front glass wall, can we suddenly fold back into the spiral by making a 180-degree turn, which echoes the two 180-degree turns already required to enter the Barcelona Pavilion. Just as Mies narrowed the entrance down, subtly constraining the visitor with a folded path, SANAA spins and squeezes the visitor between the narrow planes of acrylic that curve around until suddenly one is inside, facing the two Barcelona chairs, or rather the chairs are facing us, as if the king and queen were still there, sitting down, presiding over everything (15).

But what do they mean that the space of the pavilion is "undisturbed"? Something has changed. In fact, everything seems to have changed. The simple spiral makes a new pavilion out of the old one—a pavilion inside a pavilion, each transforming the other to produce a whole new architecture. The most famous pavilion of the twentieth century becomes something else. All the classic images embedded in the brain of every architect now have additional layers of reflections.

SANAA returns the curtain to the pavilion, or is it the pavilion to the curtain? The acrylic freestanding curtain recalls the Velvet and Silk Café a brilliant collaborative work of Lilly Reich and Mies for the exhibition *Die Mode der Dame* in Berlin, two years before Barcelona, where draperies in black, orange, and red velvet and black and yellow lemon silk hung from metal rods to form the space. The café is a kind of prototype of the pavilion, in its radical approach to defining the space by suspending sensuous surfaces. In the pavilion the richly veined marble surfaces take over the role of the curtains—the hard surfaces absorbing softness. In fact, Mies pretends that they are curtains, denying that they have a structural role, even if we now know they did. That the walls are curtains may also explain why we don't enter the Barcelona Pavilion frontally, but at an angle, as if entering behind a curtain on a stage.

SANAA's project reminds us that the Barcelona Pavilion comes from curtains, from a soft material. The beginnings of architecture were textile. It is a Semperian idea of architecture. The space that SANAA has wrapped with the new transparent curtain is precisely the center of the pavilion, the throne room, the space where the king and queen of Spain were supposed to sit and sign the book. In old pictures the space is marked by a black carpet on the floor, which nobody dares to step in, as in the photograph of the mysterious woman (is she Lilly Reich?) standing outside its border, her back to the camera, looking in. SANAA's curtain is the invisible cloak that further protects that space—a royal transparent cloak. The garment moves. It billows outward, allowing us to enter between its folds. Space is defined in a kind of invisible movement, neither limited nor unlimited, a paradox that the spiral has always communicated.

SANAA's diaphanous curtain preserves the pavilion by allowing it to breathe. It is a kind of life support in a moment in which the subtlety of Mies might so easily be forgotten precisely because the building is so insistently celebrated. The single curtain slows us down, allowing us to enter the pavilion again, as if on the day of its opening. Once again, the fact that Mies did so little, when asked to do so much (represent Germany in Barcelona), can be appreciated. Yet what allows SANAA to take us back, or bring the pavilion again forward toward us, is that the curtain is precisely not transparent. What is added is not a clear window but a delicate veil. SANAA's acrylic, like its glass, is never neutral.

SANAA's vision is far from crystal clear. In fact, its architecture appears to be more interested in blurring the view, and softening the focus, than sustaining the transparency of early avant-garde architecture. If Sejima is the inheritor of Miesian transparency, the latest in a long line of experiments, she is the ultimate Miesian, deepening the logic of transparency into a whole new kind of mirage effect. The temporary acrylic curtain in Barcelona intensifies the Miesian effect. A plastic lens is placed inside a glass lens to intensify and therefore prolong the Miesian effect, the masque of modern architecture.

The ghost here is unambiguously modern architecture, preserved rather than transformed by subtle deflections. Manifesto has gone from loud battle cry to almost silent preservation. The heroic image is preserved by an anti-heroic act: a new kind of manifesto.

Blogging Polemics

The arrival of this new kind of soft manifesto might be the endgame of the twentieth-century manifesto—the endgame of print and pavilions as the vehicles for the architectural manifesto. In an age in which electronic media is a primary site of debate and exhibition, new forms of manifesto are surely emerging.

Once again, as with the early avant-garde manifestos forged in, about, and as battle, war is the primal context. Before they were stopped, soldiers in Iraq had been uploading their videos of war on YouTube and WikiLeaks. If World War I was the first media war and Vietnam the first televised war, the war in Iraq is the first Internet, YouTube, and WikiLeaks war. Journalists are no longer the first ones on the scene, or the most captivating. Think about the blogger Riverbend, a young Iraqi woman who from 2003 to 2007, when her family moved to Syria in exasperation, reported on the day-to-day life in Iraq under the occupation in a blog called "Baghdad Burning." Or think about "CBFTW" ("Colby Buzzell Fuck the War"), the firsthand account of war in the blog of an American soldier posted in Mosul, Iraq, in 2004. The blog lasted only a few weeks before the Army forced him to close it. These blogs have told us more about the war than any other forms of traditional media.

The audience is now itself the journalist, the critic, the artist. Soldiers in Iraq shoot and edit their videos, add music to them, and so on. Riverbend's blogs have been published as a book that was translated into many languages and received many prizes. It has also been dramatized in several plays and in a BBC series. Colby Buzzell published his blogs as a book and became a writer for *Esquire* magazine. New media occupies and transforms old media. The Internet feeds new kinds of journalism, new kinds of literature, new forms of theater, new kinds of video art. Can architecture be far behind?

While most architects are still using the techniques developed by Le Corbusier and others in the wake of World War I, a new generation of architects is experimenting with a new set of media. It is perhaps this reality that makes looking at the twentieth-century little magazines and manifestos current again. As Marshall McLuhan said, every new technology makes us aware of the old one.

Le Corbusier and Mies were fascinated by the latest media and used it as a true site of architectural production. In so doing, they brought architecture into the twentieth century with a manifesto blitz. In recent years, an unexpected revolution of at least the same significance as the one that brought us photography, film, illustrated magazines, and modern publicity has taken place. The Internet, email, blogs, Google, Twitter, YouTube, Facebook, WikiLeaks, and the like have profoundly changed the way we work, write, analyze, theorize, socialize, interact, play, make love. Can we expect architecture not to be affected?

60

1   Caroline Tisdall and Angelo Bozzolla, *Futurism* (New York and Toronto: Oxford University Press, 1978).

2   Reyner Banham, *Theory and Design in the First Machine Age* (New York: Praeger, 1967), 88–89.

3   "Architektur" and "Ornament und Verbrechen" were published in French in abridged versions in *Les Cahiers d'aujourd'hui* 2 (December 1912) and 5 (June 1913), respectively. "Ornament und Verbrechen" was reprinted again in French in *L'Esprit nouveau* in 1920, while Paul Dermée, a Dadaist poet, was still part of the editorial board. *L'Esprit nouveau* announced the publication of "Architektur" in a forthcoming issue but never carried it out. The article was published in French again in *L'Architecture vivante*, (Autumn/Winter 1923): 26–34.

4   Rosalind Krauss, "The Photographic Conditions of Surrealism," *October* 19 (Winter 1981): 15–17.

5   Reyner Banham, "Zoom Wave Hits Architecture," *New Society* (3 March 1964): 21.

6   "History Is What Is Happening Today," *G: Material zur Elementaren Gestaltung*, no. 5–6 (April 1926). English translation in Detlef Mertins and Michael W. Jennings, eds., *G: An Avant-garde Journal of Art, Architecture, Design, and Film 1923–1926* (Los Angeles: Getty Research Institute, 2010), 229.

7   Incidentally an accompanying manifesto to the exhibition entitled "Vers une construction collective" was distributed during the exhibition and then published in *De Stijl*, signed by Theo van Doesburg, Cornelis Van Eesteren, and Gerrit Rietveld.

8   Mies signed the manifesto "Bauen" with his initials, M.v.d.R., and the more technical text underneath it with Mies v. d. Rohe. It is curious that he felt the need to sign twice when historians claim he wrote the text with Hans Richter, whose signature does not appear.

9   Sandra Honey, "Mies in Germany," in *Mies van der Rohe: European Works* (London: Academy Editions, 1986), 14 and 25 (note 14); David Spaeth, "Ludwig Mies van de Rohe: A Biographical Essay," in John Zukowsky, ed., *Mies Reconsidered: His Career, Legacy and Disciples* (Chicago: The Art Institute of Chicago, 1986), 15.

10   "At some point in late 1925 or early 1926, Mies directed his assistant Sergius Ruegenberg to climb to the attic of his studio at Am Karlsbad 24 and destroy all the old plans and drawings that had been stored there." Wolf Tegethoff, "From Obscurity to Maturity," in Franz Schulze, ed., *Mies van der Rohe: Critical Essays* (New York: The Museum of Modern Art, 1989), 33.

11   Philip Johnson, *Mies van der Rohe* (New York: The Museum of Modern Art, 1978; originally published 1947), 208.

12   Ibid., 211.

13   The exhibition was organized by Walter Gropius for the Arbeitsrat für Kunst. Sandra Honey, "Who and What Inspired Mies van der Rohe in Germany," in *Architectural Design*, 3/4 (1979), 99; and "Mies in Germany," in Honey, 16.

14   Mies van der Rohe in an interview with Ulrich Conrads, Berlin 1966 ("Mies in Berlin" [LP], in *Bauwelt Archiv*, 1), quoted by Honey, 16.

15   As director of the Jena Kunstverein, Walter Dexel had organized an exhibition of modern German architecture (*Neue deutsche Baukunst*, 1924), which included the Brick Country House and other projects by Mies. Wolf Tegethoff, "From Obscurity to Maturity," 57–58.

16   Julius Posener, "Los primeros años: de Schinkel a De Stijl," in *A&V: Monografías de Arquitectura y Vivienda* 6 (special issue on Mies van der Rohe, 1986): 33.

17   Rem Koolhaas and Bruce Mau, *S, M, L, XL* (New York: The Monacelli Press, 1995), 49.

18   OMA/Office for Metropolitan Architecture, "La Casa Palestra," in *AA Files* 13 (1987): 8.

ANONYMOUS MANIFESTOS

THE EYE OF THE ARCHITECT

RUBÉN A. ALCOLEA & HÉCTOR GARCÍA-DIEGO

WHEN IN 1928 the Cubo-Futurist photographer Johannes Molzahn enthusiastically commanded, "Stop reading! Look!," he anticipated one of the principles that profoundly marked the development of the artistic avant-gardes. As one of the most remarkable statements by this artist and photographer, author of the renowned *Buchkinema* or *Cinematographic Book*, it constitutes an interesting defense of visual and subjective perception over theoretical statements and exhortations. Far from an isolated example—other well-known parallels include László Moholy-Nagy's *Malerei, Fotografie, Film* (1925) or Dziga Vertov's *Der Mann mit der Kamera* (1929)—photography and cinema are defined here as a tool for expanding human perception.

These are only two examples from the immense list of writings that commonly went by the name of *manifesto* during the twentieth century, a genre understood as a public and often impassioned mission statement. The germ of the manifesto is often found in the political realm, in documents such as Karl Marx and Friedrich Engels's *Communist Manifesto* (1848), or Anselme Bellegarrigue's *Anarchist Manifesto* (1850). Nor does it seem too far-fetched to note less polemical writings such as Simón Bolívar's *Manifiesto de Cartagena* (1812), the United States Declaration of Independence (1776), or even *Plakkaat van Verlatinghe* (1581), which constituted the formal document by which the Netherlands became independent of the Spanish Crown under Philip II.

One of the greatest difficulties in reaching a consensus about the term *manifesto* is the heterogeneous and broad content of all these works, especially those that have artistic connotations. Therefore it is difficult to classify the different texts considered relevant in the twentieth century, in particular if we pay attention only to their explicit content, disregarding the underlying messages that are not directly included in the text.

Returning to Molzahn's exhortation, what constitutes the essence of the manifesto does not seem to be the text itself (this being especially pertinent when the realm extends beyond the political and delves into the artistic disciplines). The graphic power of the image has played a fundamental role in these so-called manifestos. Their authors have been fully conscious of the persuasive power of the image over the word, which enjoys a freedom of interpretation and communication well beyond the barriers of language. Indeed, certain images have arguably been more influential than the texts they accompanied. The images shown in *Vers une architecture* (1923), for example, persist in the collective memory more clearly than the texts they followed, and announced with great clarity the main arguments and ideas beyond the book, functioning independently of the text they illustrated.

Although many of the architectural manifestos that appeared during the twentieth century were conceived of as manifestos, it is the nature of architecture culture that we have interpreted many essays as manifestos *a posteriori,* by including them, often by chance, in historical texts that analyze the broad spectrum of theoretical contributions to architecture.[1] Whether the texts had the clear intention of being a manifesto from the beginning, or later transcended the initial expectations of their authors by being read in this way, the truth is that all of them have in common the use of the image as an essential support for discourse, even occasionally playing the main role.

On this matter, it is possible to note a dramatic change in attitude after 1920, the influence of which extends until today. It was during those years, under the shadow of the fusion of art and technique, that deep transformations in the theory of perception developed, yielding fantastic and renowned essays and publications praising modernity. One of these books is *Amerika: Bilderbuch eines Architekten* (1926), produced by Erich Mendelsohn after returning from a trip to the United States (a book that El Lissitzky and Alexander Rodchenko considered the beginning of an era of a new vision).[2]

Beyond the visual revolution, often linked to the consolidation of photography as the main vehicle for broadcasting modernism, it is possible to sense something deeper: the autonomy of the image, which came to define the photo-manifesto as a specific category distinct from the traditional classifications of canonical texts. Parallel to the linear reading of the text, an impressionistic interpretation of photographs and drawings used by architects allows us to foretell, against what might seem obvious, the most essential and deep interpretation of the modern postulates. Avoiding here a deep or difficult semiotic discourse, we might simply look to the most famous arguments of Gestalt theory, which provided a model for the interpretation of the image as a totally autonomous sign.[3] If image had been historically subordinated to text, as example or illustration, the avant-gardes were able to provide it with an autonomous or even predominant role, radically reversing the process. Until that time, it was possible to choose among different photographs to illustrate a particular idea, associating image with text. Modernity, however, proposed a complete dissociation of written and visual languages. It is in this way that the so common systematic repetition of the same image in different works obtains a meaning beyond the morbid exercise of finding duplicated photographs in that same or different architecture. Thus, Ludwig Hilberseimer on several occasions in his *Großstadtarchitektur* (1927), used photographs that had been published before by Richard Neutra in his *Wie baut Amerika?* (1927), some of which were also used by Erich Mendelsohn in *Russland, Europa, Amerika* (1929), which constituted a sort of a second part of his *Amerika*.[4]

Mendelsohn's manner of reusing photographs is especially meaningful. The only picture appearing in *Russland, Europa, Amerika* that recalls his earlier interest in American silos comes directly from his first book, *Amerika: Bilderbuch eines Architekten*, although Mendelsohn frames and enlarges the image to show a specific area (making the original almost unrecognizable) (1, 2). This same formula would be used on a number of different occasions throughout the book. The photograph illustrating a New York street in *Amerika*, captioned *Nebenstrasse* (Side Street) also appears blown up and cropped—leaving out the parked vehicles in *Russland, Europa, Amerika* (3, 4). The same thing happens in still another picture of Fifth Avenue, which in *Amerika* is seen in a very general view, but in *Russland, Europa, Amerika* becomes almost unrecognizable because of the way Mendelsohn enlarges and frames it (5, 6).[5] Both books are fundamentally visual, in the manner of the very commercially successful photographic books published by Rudolf Mosse in Berlin.[6]

If *Amerika* presents a visual record of Mendelsohn's journey to the United States, *Russland, Europa, Amerika* goes beyond that, directly comparing and contrasting visions of different territories. Images from Russia portray popular and traditional architecture, in contrast to America, which is pictured through images of large-scale constructions, especially Mendelsohn's beloved skyscrapers. Europe meanwhile is presented as a place of emerging ideas and intellectual concerns, conveyed through images of housing projects and numerous drawings of unbuilt projects. The introduction, written by Mendelsohn, makes it clear that the intention is to synthetically portray the cultural reality of an era. In his words, the book "is not about politics; but both politics and business are the solid pillars that support architecture, so in the confrontation of Russia against Europe and America the most decisive and deep problems and the most elevated realities are tackled." As in *Amerika*, every image is placed "in its specific position, besides a dense text with a constant rhythm," producing an effect that is partway between aesthetic manifesto and cinematographic tracking shot.[7]

Mendelsohn's example is paradigmatic, but it is not the only one. The realm of architectural publishing during these years revolved around a formulation of a new architecture that was presented mainly through images. In 1926, *Das Werk* included an article by Hannes Meyer titled

"Die neue Welt" in which, after a brief introduction about art and life, Meyer included a visual sequence grouped with titles such as "The Cinema," "The Image," or "Propaganda."[8] Within this sequence, he devoted a section

1 Photograph of grain silos in Erich Mendelsohn, *Russland, Europa, Amerika* (1929), 19; enlarged and cropped from *Amerika*.

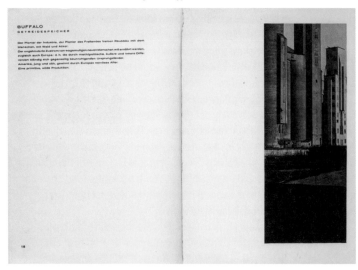

2 Photograph of grain silos in Erich Mendelsohn, *Amerika* (1926), 37. The location is listed as Chicago, which will be corrected to Buffalo in *Russland, Europa, Amerika*.

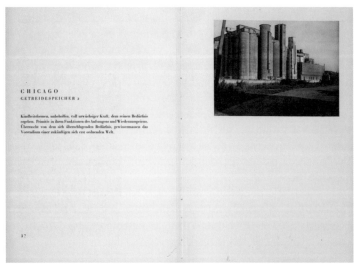

to modern books and magazines, quoting from heavily illustrated books by authors such as Le Corbusier, Theo van Doesburg, El Lissitzky, Ludwig Hilberseimer, Kurt Schwitters, and Adolf Behne.

3 Photograph of Fifth Avenue, New York, in Erich Mendelsohn, *Amerika* (1926), 50.

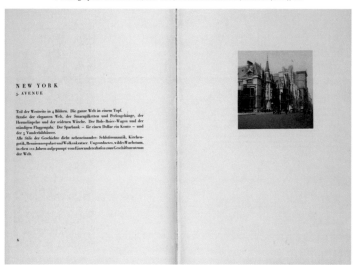

4 Photograph of Fifth Avenue, New York, in Erich Mendelsohn, *Russland, Europa, Amerika* (1929), 13; enlarged and cropped from *Amerika*.

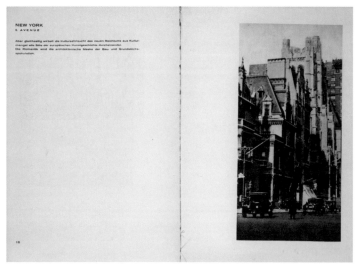

Many of the images and photographs published in these visual catalogues went on to enjoy independent afterlives, subsequently being republished in a number of books. However, the autonomy of the photographs from the original texts that accompanied the images is expressed

5 Photograph of side street, New York in Erich Mendelsohn, *Amerika* (1926), 6.

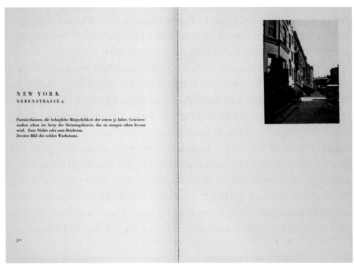

6 Photograph of side street, New York, in Erich Mendelsohn, *Russland, Europa, Amerika* (1929), 17; enlarged and cropped from *Amerika*.

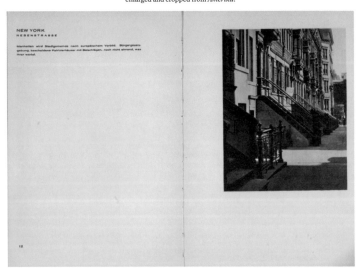

not only through systematic repetition but also through the subtleties offered by photography that went beyond the architectural description. We might recall, for example, a photograph of a house by Karl Schneider published in Adolf Behne's *Neues Wohnen, Neues Bauen* (1927), displaying, among other subtleties, the interaction of architecture and landscape (7). In turn, that same house was used by Walter Gropius in his *Internationale Architektur* (1925) and presented as an example of an autonomous and abstract object composed simply of two brick cubes (8). Two images ascribed opposite intentions to the same architectural work.[9]

Other architects turned directly to photographers or typographers to design the interior of their books, turning them into composition exercises in which every element was designed with a visual intention. Sigfried Giedion collaborated with Moholy-Nagy to design the interior of his famous *Bauen in Frankreich, Bauen in Eisen, Bauen in Eisenbeton* (1928), even against the opposition of the publisher.[10] Something similar happened with Bruno Taut, who entrusted Johannes Molzahn with the design not only of the cover but also the interior of his *Bauen: Der neue Wohnbau* (1927).[11] Molzahn's radical work led him to voluntarily unbalance the composition of certain pages, especially those referring to traditional architecture, often with derisive descriptions such as "it is not cardboard" or "style salad."

7 Karl Schneider, Haus Michaelsen, near Blankenese outside of Hamburg, Germany, in Adolf Behne, *Neus Wohnen, Neues Bauen* (1927), 116.

116

Dieses Haus steht in Blankenese, das Stendhal einen der drei schönsten Punkte Europas nannte. Der Blick in das breite Elbtal ist in der Tat wunderbar. Der Architekt hat das Haus auf das engste mit der Landschaft verbunden. Einfachste Formen und Flächen, klarer, logisch bewegter Körper, mächtige Fensteröffnungen zum Strom, unzerrissene Rasenflächen. Das Barrierenlose ist schön an diesem Bau.

The pages devoted to modern architecture, by contrast, were composed as double-page spreads with a unified, perfectly balanced layout, and included high-quality photographs and references to standardization. The way the interior of the book is laid out is not incidental either; considering the double page as a single unified spread was something very common in these visual books about architecture. The image of architecture conveyed by the layout goes beyond the limits of the photographic illustration of buildings to create an integrated whole with the text, perceived at a glance, and conceptually linked to the widespread practice of photomontage used in graphics in Central Europe and elsewhere.

The predominance of increasingly graphic layouts over literary discourse produced a whole new genre in architectural literature. In many cases the intention of their authors reflected a certain eagerness to display a finished, homogeneous, and specific image of the intentions or arguments transmitted. This more visual way to develop ideas offered fewer constraints to better explain the formal and compositional arguments some

8 Karl Schneider, Haus Michaelsen, near Blankenese outside of Hamburg, Germany, in Walter Gropius, *Internationale Architektur* (1925), 71.

KARL SCHNEIDER, Hamburg, — Haus Michaelsen, Falkenstein a. d. Elbe, bei Hamburg. Backstein gekalkt. 1923

ANONYMOUS MANIFESTOS

architects wanted to achieve than, in many cases, elaborate complicated texts or abstruse reasoning. In short, all these manifesto-catalogues are composed of a large number of images brought together with a brief text that serves as a support or accompaniment and which, in some instances, can even be disregarded. In this way, the narration is composed of many different layers, allowing for readings at different levels, from the most superficial or banal to a reading linked to the most profound of the aesthetic categories of modernity's visual principles.

It is obvious that the morphology of all of these visual manifestos refers to the great photographic albums that became so popular in bourgeois culture at the turn of the century, such as the ones that collected pictures from distant cities or cultures. In them, the indelible footprint synthesizing the essential was grouped as a single object. The sum of all these ephemeral and fleeting experiences has turned contradictorily into categorical invariants close to the unchangeable and therefore purposeful. Moholy-Nagy's or Molzahn's arguments seem to be found in other texts of that same era, even if these are apparently alien to their immediate circle of reference. Sigmund Freud referred to the double nature of photography in an essay from 1930, seeing it as a comprehensive recording method but also purposeful and instrumental: "The photographic camera has been created as an instrument which retains the fleeting visual impressions, just as the gramophone disc retains the equally fleeting auditory ones; both are at bottom materializations of the power he possesses of recollection, his memory."[12]

Every single one of the image collections presented in these architecture books becomes, in itself, an eloquent partial or autobiographical stock list of the plastic and theoretical interests of their authors. And as a whole, it constitutes a visual universe of the principles that would go on to become common references. The manifesto is made up of the aggregation of individual visual elements, and, differing from other speculative arguments, the interpretation is neither direct nor imposed, leaving all responsibility to the reader. Alberto Sartoris's encyclopedic work *Gli elementi dell'architettura funzionale* (1932) might be a good example of this. Assembling over a thousand photographs of different projects and buildings scattered around the world, Sartoris attempted to offer a panoramic vision of the essence of modern architecture.[13] Sartoris's subtitle, *Sintesi panoramica dell'architettura moderna* (Panoramic Synthesis of Modern Architecture), is expressive enough of this ambition. A brief introductory text with many images announcing the aforementioned characteristic elements of the modern works is followed by an almost infinite-seeming sequence of images, to complete the nearly one thousand pages that make up the book—a panoramic synthesis indeed. Something similar happens with the monumental series of three volumes *Neues Bauen in der Welt* (1930), produced by the renowned publisher Joseph Gantner. With the aim of consolidating and internationalizing the concepts, he relied heavily on photography, producing three exceptional books devoted to Russia, America, and France, compiled by El Lissitzky, Richard Neutra, and Robert Ginsburger, respectively.[14]

The visual catalogue is thus turned into a type of manifesto, more focused on the ideas that come through our vision to our deep unconscious, and in which authorship vanishes gradually. This does not rely on the authentic or original generation of each picture, in terms of authorship, but on the synthetic capacity of grouping, rearranging, repeating, or manipulating those images that are already part of the collective imagination. The singularity or unique authenticity of the architectural work transforms into a collage in which images and architecture displace their authors.

The intended anonymous American architecture displayed by Mendelsohn in his books, through the recycling of images and fragments, or the voluminous photographic catalogues by Bruno Taut or Alberto Sartoris are, despite an obvious distance in terms of time and context, not far from the underlying conceptual principles of Bernard Rudofsky's famous 1964 exhibition at the Museum of Modern Art (MoMA) titled *Architecture Without Architects*. The exhibition's catalogue offered almost two hundred photographs presenting the work of anonymous builders in completely disparate places. It is not by chance that the catalogue would sometimes be viewed as a "perfectly suitable substitute" for the exhibition, making the visit to the exhibition redundant.[15] For the exhibition and catalogue, Rudofsky used images from a number of varied sources such as anthropological archives or diplomatic and military departments, as well as some photographs he had taken himself during the late 1920s. It was on his trips through Italy in this period that he collected the pictures he would later characterize as "imaginative photographs taken by architects or photographers with a keen eye for modern architecture."[16] It is also not by chance that some of these images had been previously shown in the 1930 exhibition *Deutsche Bauausstellung Berlin*, anticipating the 1964 MoMA exhibition of "spontaneous architecture."

Although the exhibition has been seen as a critique of orthodox "International Style" architecture, it was also linked with its deepest statements. Rudofsky uses the same tools and methods, elaborating a visual catalogue rather than a simple exhibition, one whose influence extended well beyond the scarce four months the exhibition was on view at MoMA. The number of editions of the catalogue published over twenty-five years, along with the dozens of countries where the exhibition was displayed, attest to how the exhibition became a sort of universal photo-manifesto. We see an endless succession of photographs, with barely any text, encompassing everything from an indigenous Alaskan igloo to the mud and stone skyscrapers of Yemen, to Galician elevated stone *hórreos* or Castilian castles.

Rudofsky's use of the most radical and modern structure, the photo-manifesto, as a means of expression and critique of the avant-garde's principles opens the door to a new category or, at least, an alternative classification. The compendium of images, generally used in a banal manner in postmodernity, was a symbolic (and perhaps the only possible) way of transmitting the deepest and most essential derivations of modernity. Such compendia begin to play a metaphorical role, suggesting something that is beyond what is photographed or intended by their authors, and become discourses that, as suggested by Minor White, "use the camera in relation to the mind, the heart, viscera and spirit of human beings. The perennial trend has barely been started in photography."[17]

73

1   See Ulrich Conrads, *Programs and Manifestoes on 20th Century Architecture* (Cambridge, MA: The MIT Press, 1970); Joan Ockman, *Architecture Culture, 1943-1968: A Documentary Anthology* (New York: Rizzoli International Publications, 1993); K. Michael Hays, *Architecture Theory since 1968* (Cambridge, MA: The MIT Press, 1998); and Panayotis Tournikiotis, *The Historiography of Modern Architecture* (Cambridge, MA: The MIT Press, 1999). We can also mention Spanish efforts, such as Pere Hereu, Josep María Montaner, and Jordi Oliveras, *Textos de arquitectura de la modernidad* (Madrid: Nerea, 1994); and Simón Marchan, *La arquitectura del siglo XX* (Madrid: Corazón, 1974).

2   Erich Mendelsohn, *Amerika: Bilderbuch eines Architekten: Mit 100 meis eigenen Aufnahmen des Verfassers* (Berlin: Rudolf Mosse 1926); see also Matthias Noell, "Nicht mehr lesen! Sehen! Le livre d'architecture de langue allemande dans les années vingt," in Jean-Michel Leniaud and Béatrice Bouvier, *Le livre d'architecture XVe-XXe siècle: Edition, représentations et bibliothèques* (Paris: Ecole des Chartes, 2002).

3   See also Lucía Santaella and Winfried Nöth, *Imagen: Comunicación, semiótica y medios* (Kassel: Reichenberg, 2003); and Rene Lindekens, *Elements pour une sémiotique de la photographie* (Paris: Didier, 1971), 38-58.

4   Ludwig Hilberseimer, *Großstadtarchitektur* (Stuttgart: Julius Hoffmann,1927); Richard J. Neutra, *Wie baut Amerika?: Gegenwärtige Bauarbeit amerikanischer Kreis* (Stuttgart: Julius Hoffmann,1927); Erich Mendelsohn, *Russland, Europa, Amerika; Ein architektonischer Querschnitt* (Berlin: Rudolf Mosse, 1929).

5   These are just two examples, but there are many others. The photograph published on page 19 in *Russland, Europa, Amerika*, is a partial view of the image published on page 37 in *Amerika*; also, the pictures in pages 13 and 17 in *Russland, Europa, Amerika*, are details of the pictures published on pages 6 and 50 in *Amerika*.

6   Notable, for example, is a book by Hans Hildebrant that, in 337 images, systematically illustrated artistic contributions made by women.

See Hans Hildebrant, *Die Frau als Künstlerin, mit 337 Abbildungen nach frauenarteiten bildender Kunst von der frühesten Zeiten bis zur Gegenwart* (Berlin: Rudolf Mosse, 1928).

7   Mendelsohn, *Russland, Europa, Amerika*, foreword (n.p.).

8   Hannes Meyer, "Die neue Welt," in *Das Werk* (1926): 205-236. See also Bruno Maurer, "Das Werk," *Architese* 5, no. 24 (1995): 17-29.

9   Adolf Behne, *Neues Wohnen, Neues Bauen* (Leipzig: Hesse & Becker, 1927), 116; Walter Gropius, *Internationale Architektur* (Munich: Albert Langen, 1925), 66.

10   Sigfried Giedion, *Bauen in Frankreich, Bauen in Eisen, Bauen in Eisenbeton* (Leipzig and Berlin: Klinkhardt & Biermann, 1928).

11   Bruno Taut, *Bauen: Der neue Wohnbau* (Leipzig and Berlin: Klinkhardt & Biermann, 1927).

12   Sigmund Freud, *Das Unbehagen in der Kultur* (Vienna: Internationaler Psychoanalytischer Verlag, 1930). Published in English as Sigmund Freud, *Civilization and Its Discontents* (New York: W. W. Norton, 1962), 38.

13   Alberto Sartoris, *Gli elementi dell'architettura funzionale: Sintesi panoramica dell'architettura moderna* (Milan: Ulrico Hoepli, 1932).

14   El Lissitzky, *Russland: Die Rekonstruktion der Architektur in der Sowietunion, Neues Bauen in der Welt*, no. 1 (Vienna: Anton Schroll & Co., 1930); Richard J. Neutra, *Amerika: Die Stilbildung des neuen Bauens in den Vereinigten Staaten, Neues Bauen in der Welt*, no. 2 (Vienna: Anton Schroll & Co., 1930); and Robert Ginsburger, *Frankreich: Die Entwicklung der neuen Ideen nach Konstruktion und Form, Neues Bauen in der Welt*, no. 3 (Vienna: Anton Schroll & Co., 1930).

15   Felicity Scott, "An Eye for Modern Architecture," in *Lessons from Bernard Rudofsky: Life as a Voyage*, Architektur Zentrum Wien, ed., (Basel: Birkhauser, 2007), 175.

74

ANONYMOUS MANIFESTOS

16   Bernard Rudofsky, Letter to Luis Sert (September 25, 1982), cited in Scott, "An Eye for Modern Architecture," 176.

17   Minor White, "Equivalence: The Perennial Trend," *PSA Journal* 29, no. 7 (1963): 17–21.

THE ALHAMBRA PALACE, THE KATSURA OF THE WEST

A STONE MANIFESTO

JOSÉ MANUEL POZO &
JOSÉ ÁNGEL MEDINA

Give him alms, woman,
for there is nothing sadder in life
than being blind in Granada

—Francisco Alarcón de Icaza

"THE ALHAMBRA WILL UNDOUBTEDLY CONTINUE to provide humanity with an essential wellspring of beauty," the Spanish architect Carlos Jiménez recently wrote.[1] In these few words, with their simple yet sensitive expression, Jiménez captured a principle that would prove obvious to any careful observer of this architectural monument. The same sensory evidence of that beauty, however, can become an obstacle to perceiving the invisible attributes it possesses—the determinant values that turn this palace into a true stone manifesto of perennial value, as Jiménez pointed out.

If, instead, we are distracted by its prepossessing appearance or the decoration of its surfaces (outstanding though they may be), or if we simply regard the structure as an eminent relic or incomparable evidence of the artistic wisdom of an ancient time—from its origins in the year 889 across the centuries of its construction—we would miss what is most important about the Alhambra. That is what cannot be perceived with the senses but must be perceived with the mind: the intellectual vision announced by Goethe when he asserted that "those who can only appreciate an experience do not understand that the experience is only half of an experience."[2]

Much has been written—and will continue to be written—about Granada's Alhambra, one of the most outstanding jewels of Hispano-Arabic culture (and indeed the whole of Islamic art), and there is much to say about its construction, character, and evolution. But it has not necessarily been considered in terms of what it represents for the qualities of contemporary architecture worldwide, and in Spain in particular. Its past, its appearance, and its history have been widely studied, but little attention has been paid to its essence, to which it owes its past and future importance (as well as its touristic and historical significance) and its seductive beauty.

The Alhambra is unique in the Western world, yet finds its parallel in another palace with which it shares many elements and which has been considered an early materialization of modern architecture: the Katsura Imperial Villa in Kyoto, Japan (1). The wonder and admiration that traditional Japanese architecture aroused in Walter Gropius is well known, and led him to write the following enthusiastic words to Le Corbusier: "Dear Corbu, all what we have been fighting for has its parallel in old Japanese culture. This rock-garden of Zen monks in the thirteenth century—stones and raked white pebbles—an elating spot of peace. You would be as excited as I am in this 2,000-year-old space of cultural wisdom!"[3] However, in spite of the enthusiasm and sincerity of the words used by Gropius to recognize his surprise and, implicitly, his prior ignorance of Katsura, we can attribute only an indirect effect on the work of Gropius himself and that of his contemporaries—at least *a posteriori*.

Mark Wigley's astute observations concerning Jørn Utzon's travels during the development of his Sydney Opera House project (and his "discovery" of Japanese and other national architectures during his travels) shed some light on why this might be so. Wigley recalls the typical journey of the interested and thoughtful architect, during which the architect discovers what he was really looking for—something that he somehow already knew, of course, and that is why he ends up finding it. Therefore what the traveler actually does is recognize "what he already knows" rather than discover it.[4] Undoubtedly, Gropius's first trip to the East was one of these journeys,

1 Yasuhiro Ishimoto, photograph of Japanese stone garden, Ryoanji Temple at Katsura Imperial Villa. From *Katsura: Tradition and Creation in Japanese Architecture* (1960).

Stone Garden (Ryoanji Temple)

THE ALHAMBRA PALACE, KATSURA OF THE WEST

one of recognition and confirmation of what he already knew rather than of discovery; and if we pay attention to the strong Eastern backdrop *ex origine* that can be associated with modern abstraction (as I have recently tried to point out in another context) we could probably make this claim for Gropius's journeys even more strongly than we can for Utzon's.[5]

The Katsura Palace and its gardens became an evocative, dreamy Arcadia for the most refined and vanguard architects, and an iconic reference for modern architecture, which saw the palace as a paradigm of formal and constructive ideals (2). The spaces and gardens of the Alhambra possess similar qualities. For this reason the architecture of the Alhambra is also present, consciously or unconsciously, in many of the achievements of Western architecture of the twentieth century and especially in Spanish architecture. As in the case of Katsura, this results not from the seduction that its shapes or its decoration have exercised as a source of inspiration, but from its abstract qualities and the strength of its "soul"—what Spanish architect Fernando Chueca Goitia tried to portray and propose as a model for his contemporaries with the Manifesto of the Alhambra (*Manifiesto de*

2 Katsura Imperial Villa, overall plan. From *Katsura: Tradition and Creation in Japanese Architecture.*

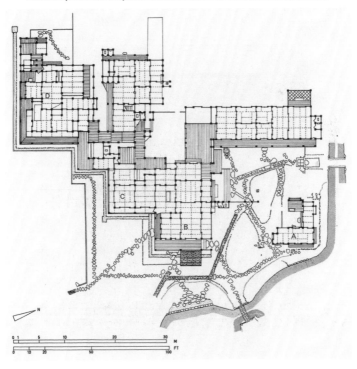

la Alhambra), published in 1953.[6] (3) The document was the result of a gathering of architects who sought lessons for contemporary practice in this monument of the past, and the significance of the manifesto lies not so much in its content as in the search encouraged by its writing and the determination of the architects who arrived in Granada in 1952, of which the essay is merely an external symbol.

Therefore we should be interested in knowing what those architects were looking for, and what they found in the process of writing the manifesto itself—and if any of that still has relevance today. At the same time, and almost as a response to these questions, we might ask ourselves if what the Alhambra offered could not be found elsewhere. It is clear that the selection of the palace was not accidental, as evidenced by two other parallel enterprises that emerged almost simultaneously and sought a new path for the advancement of Spanish architecture: one was the contemporaneous publication of Luis Moya's manifesto; the other was the formation of El Grupo R (Grup R or R Group), a group of Catalan architects headed by José Antonio Coderch, Josep Maria Sostres, and Oriol Bohigas. None of these figures were in Granada in 1952, although they shared with those who attended Chueca's meeting the desire to find a new way for architecture.

In the early 1950s, and perhaps not by chance coinciding with Spain's acceptance into the United Nations, Spanish architects were

3 *Manifiesto de la Alhambra* (1953).

THE ALHAMBRA PALACE, KATSURA OF THE WEST

already aware that in order to contribute to the progress of their society, it was necessary to find a new direction for their work and for architectural education. Isolated because of two wars—a civil war followed by a foreign conflict—the country had been immersed in two decades of disconnection from the international cultural, political, and economic world. The isolation had been no less in architecture, producing an understandable introversion that turned to history for the stability and excellence that it was lacking, as stated in the introduction of the *Manifesto of the Alhambra*: "Spain had to retrieve its greatness; thus it seems fair that it would dress itself with the splendors of an imperial past... It was not the fury, the peculiarity, nor the traditional leanings that were the concern; it was the hieratic character, the gravity, the immobile majesty of politics that needed to be restored. We kept on, as we keep on."[7]

The aforementioned Moya, who was by this time an intellectual authority in Spain, did not want to join in the so-called Critical Sessions held at the Alhambra—where the stakes of Spanish architecture's history and future were debated—although he had attended previous meetings.[8] Moya advocated the need to maintain the forms of "Spanish classicism"— forms that were subject to his own interpretation. At the same time he despised functionalism, Le Corbusier's rationalism, Wright's organic architecture, and, in short, all modern forms and accomplishments as incorrect or wrongly built.

The Catalan architects of Grupo R, however, wanted to become the heirs of the seminal 1931 CIAM offshoot known as GATEPAC (Grupo de Artistas y Técnicos Españoles para la Arquitectura Contemporánea), by cultivating their somewhat mythicized international aesthetic. In that sense, Bohigas's optimistic interpretation of Josep Lluis Sert's Central Antituberculosis Clinic and Casa Bloc as Spain's only two strictly modern works is enlightening; for Bohigas everything else was marked by an eclecticism that started with the Alhambra. That is perhaps why Coderch—not fond of Bohigas's manners—left Grupo R even though it had been founded in his own architecture office. If Moya was searching for the support of historical vernacular tradition, Catalan architects sought to "integrate the architectural practice into the European context," as has been pointed out by the architect Juan Miguel Hernández León.[9] Thus, both the Catalan architects and Moya proposed formal models rather than conceptual ones, resulting in a brief and ephemeral form of validation.

The "alhambrinos" (as those who met in Granada in 1952 were known), or at least the core adherents, as not all of them were so adamant, sensed that the problem was deeper. It was not an issue of style, but of soul.

A timeless building, embodying optimism and vitality, the Alhambra seemed the perfect gathering place to consider a properly Spanish architecture (4). The importance of the *Manifesto of the Alhambra*, then, was its function as a wake-up call, to acknowledge the true influence and validity of Granada's palace as much greater than commonly recognized. Indeed, even as its influence became greater, it grew more difficult to specify the details of its legacy in terms of its plastic form or in the functional scheme. Its influence stems from the restoration of pre-Renaissance popular Hispano-Arabic architecture—which in many senses is the same as calling it "modern," if we think along the same lines as Wilhelm Worringer when he referred to abstraction and formal asceticism of ancient times, without the later introduction of stylistic additions.[10]

At the same time, the perception of the Alhambra as plastically eclectic, as pointed out by Bohigas, is a postive factor. Thus, the authors of the *Manifesto* saw "a great advantage for those seeking creative incentives" in the fact that "the floor plan of the Escorial Monastery could fit perfectly a ministry; while the Alhambra is perfectly useless for modern life."[11] The strength of the building lies in the fact that it serves no specific function, and this is its main virtue and the reason for its permanence: "Precisely because the Alhambra is not usable in an

4 The Alhambra, overall plan.

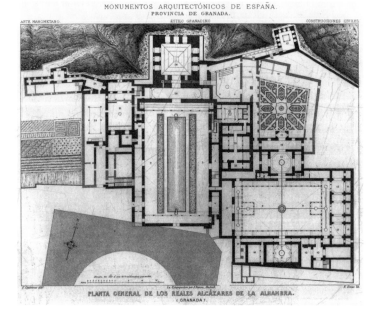

THE ALHAMBRA PALACE, KATSURA OF THE WEST

immediate way as functional architecture is the reason that we regard it with such joy."[12]

Beyond the impact that the Alhambra had on these visitors, the building encapsulates in stone and lime the essential issues of the most characteristic architecture of the twentieth century, similar to what occurred with traditional Japanese architecture, but perhaps even more clearly. We cannot consider the Nasrid dynasty palaces of the Alhambra solely as the Spanish (or Western) Katsura. The Alhambra merits the same aura of purity with which the Japanese imperial palace has been regarded, turning its architecture and gardens into even a spiritual reference. But the Alhambra has signified something else, due to its geographical position and its cultural and historical context, of which it is an eminent but not unique example.

Those meeting at the Alhambra were seeking the advice its stones could offer: they were hoping to be able to capture the centuries-old wisdom trapped within the Alhambra's walls, and from the stillness of its gardens unfold the secrets that turned the building into a monument—a monument as Louis Kahn defined it, a timeless building that goes beyond simply wealth or large size to create a sense of serenity and an adequate proportion in a given place or a given landscape.[13] This is the fundamental characteristic, allowing for a building to insert itself in the tradition of the place that hosts it, which it will later own, as a predominant element in the landscape, whether rural or urban, and regardless of its size.

Since the mid-nineteenth century, Japanese and other Orientalist tendencies had spread throughout Europe and internationally, fed partly by Romanticism and curiosity, but primarily encouraged by the aspiration to find new ways of expression for architecture that might overcome the exhaustion point reached by the increasingly eclectic Mannerism of western art. An "Alhambra" branch came out of this general trend, imitating the shapes and ornaments of the courtyards and living rooms of the Granada palace and reaching extremes we now consider grotesque. Examples of this include Owen Jones's rebuilding of the Alhambra in the second Crystal Palace (Sydenham, England, 1854); the trompe l'oeil used by a Frenchman by the name of Dermaz as the foundation of his *L'Andalousie au temps des Maures* pavilion at the 1900 Exposition Universelle in Paris; and the reproduction of the Court of the Lions in the Spanish Pavilion at the 1910 Exposition Universelle in Brussels by Modesto Cendoya, which gave way to forms inspired to a lesser or greater extent by the Alhambra in "civic" works such as the later Xifré Palace in Madrid and the "shocking" Alhambra Palace Hotel, built in 1910 by Cendoya at the heart of Grenada's Albaicín—the old Moorish quarter of the city—where its heavy, pseudo-Arabic mass still stands today.

But all these, along with many other examples that could be cited, demonstrate an inspiration based on imitation—a copy or the emulation of the formal and ornamental aspects—but not the essence of the building.[14] Thus, Cendoya copied the Court of the Lions but not how it is approached and traversed, and even altered its proportions, reducing the number of arches. This is a Mannerist Orientalism, fed by a fascination with the mystery and legend of the Alhambra itself in a sense that has nothing to do with what the writers of the *Manifesto of the Alhambra* sought when they stated, "We did not come to praise copying the Alhambra; we came for the opposite."[15]

While the taste for the exotic and Orientalism led Europe to look to the East, both near and far, in Spain this attention was directed at its own history, which possessed stunning "Oriental" examples including the Alhambra and the Great Mosque of Cordoba—but also examples of relative "orientality." This architecture was as Hispanic as the Escorial. It had indeed come from the East, in the eighth century, but as the Barbarians had come from the north only six centuries later, the two strains were perfectly merged, producing something outstanding and unique from that combination—what Mexican architect Luis Barragán would call the "wisdom of the Spanish Moors."[16]

That architecture was indigenous, as evidenced by the fact that in the sixteenth century, after the expulsion of the Moors at the end of the fifteenth century, the Palace of Charles V was built within the Alhambra complex—its residents recognizing the Alhambra as genuine Spanish architecture. The architects did not build on top of it, nor near it, nor far away from it, but rather they joined the new volume with the existing one in a continuous whole, as a tribute or an acknowledgment of the dynamics of the previous palace. The newer building was not an addition but conceived as another part of the palace. Those gathered in Granada in 1952 were aware of this, for while "in America the Japanese is something far-fetched, Arabianism in Spain is an innate component of our culture."[17] It has been Spain's great fortune in the twentieth century to possess in its own architecture a superb example that perfectly combines tradition with the claims of aesthetics, construction, and modern society. Spanish architects had only to return to their traditional principles and allow these practices to become the soul that would warm the body of architecture.

The preface to the *Manifesto of the Alhambra* expresses it as follows: "We have come to realize the modern values, in a purely architectural sense, of the Alhambra. The relation between this fourteenth-century building and the most advanced architecture is, to some extent, very apparent: they coincide in the acceptance of humanistic measure; in the asymmetric but organic composition of the floor plan; in the purity and sincerity of the resulting volumes; in the way that garden and landscape are added to the building; in the economical and strict use of materials, without ornamental 'fat,' and in many more aspects that would take too long to list."[18]

The two questions raised earlier are therefore answered: Why go to the Alhambra? What did those who went there discover? Architects went to the Alhambra for the same reason that Utzon traveled to Mexico in 1966, in Wigley's account of why architects travel: because they needed to confirm their intuitions and rehearse what they already knew. They did not actually find anything—they returned to Madrid without the text, which was written afterward. They had "remembered" many things, however: that good architecture demands humility and time to develop, never urgency; that materials should be used as they are without imitating something else or adding superfluous and banal ornaments; that symmetry was a source of great satisfaction; that diagonals significantly enriched spaces; that bare walls were rewarding; that a window was a cut in the wall and not another building; that the contrasts between light and shadow, textures, dimensions, and colors were important; that a garden and a patio should not be considered as existing only outdoors but as a substantial part of the building; that the succession of planes provides infinity and emotion to space; that the module and dimensions of a simple brick, or a *Mocárabe* (honeycomb work) can become the origin of all proportions; and, foremost, that architecture must serve man rather than man adapt to architecture (5–7).[19]

Gropius described these lessons so well that it is useful to recall his impressions of the Japanese palace here, as we consider the Alhambra Palace, its courtyards, and its gardens with water flowing through them:

> The building and its immediate surroundings constitute a homo-geneous, integrated space composition; no static conception, no symmetry, no central focus in the plan. Space, here the only medium of artistic creation, appears to be magically floating. Most characteristic of the spirit of the conception is the path to the entrance gate of the villa... There is a decided distaste for the imposing straight avenue; instead, there is a preference or the intimate and casual but carefully planned approach which supplies surprises at every turn and leads up to the main objective in a human, natural, unimposing manner.

The spirit of the design conception, particularly that of the early part of the building, the Old Shoin, is of remarkable clarity... The modular coordination used at this period was the most subtle known, more so than that of the Egyptians, even more than that of the Greeks... all the building parts were dimensioned horizontally and vertically on a multiple of the column thickness, which varied with the sizes of the spaces and their respective spans.

The living spaces are modest in size, in keeping with the human scale. The use of movable partitions and window frames makes their proportions extremely variable. The accentuated emptiness of the rooms with their subdued walls is a deliberately intended factor of design; its purpose is to put the emphasis on the human figure and support it with a sympathetic background. As in most Japanese creations, we find a predilection for clear contrasts: against the austere purity of the architectural frame, the spontaneous, sketchlike painting and the wealth of magnificent garments; against the light, transparent house construction, the heavy, sculptural roof. The use of contrasting materials which enhance each other in their effectiveness had been developed early, and nowhere does one find an attempt at "matching" by identical forms and colors (one of the American preoccupations), but always great care in complementing, relating, and counter-balancing. Man's oneness with nature is expressed by the use

5 The Alhambra, different types of stone at the carriage entry. Photograph by the author.

6 The Alhambra, east face of the Comares tower.

THE ALHAMBRA PALACE, KATSURA OF THE WEST

of materials left in their natural colors and by a love of the deliberately unfinished detail, corresponding to the irregularities in nature. For only the incomplete was considered to still be part of the fluid process of life; symmetry, the symbol of perfection, was reserved for the temple. The aesthetic effect is a pure, architectonic one, achieved by simple contrasts of bright and dark, smooth and rough and by juxtaposition of plain squares, rectangles, and stripes. However, none of these means are aesthetic abstractions; they are all meaningful realities, related to daily life. The builder subordinated himself and his work to the supra-individual idea of a unified environment and thereby avoided the traps of vanity, the *nouveauté* and the stunt. This is the lofty abode of man in equilibrium, in serenity.[20]

There is no record of Gropius ever having visited the Alhambra, but his description of the aesthetic and tectonic characteristics of the Katsura Palace are also valid for the Grenadian palace. Both works were also altered over time (8). While the Alhambra has not been rebuilt a number of times as Katsura has, following the same construction, the Alhambra has been substantially remade over time since the durability of its materials have necessitated repairs and reconstrucion of elements. Like the ship of Theseus, it remains the same. Carlos Jiménez has noted, "The Alhambra is not an escape from the world but a complex spatial sequence revealing paradise, or the one our short stay on earth can be able to build... Traveling

7 The Alhambra, passage to the Court of the Lions from the Hall of the Muqarnas. Photograph by the author.

around the Alhambra I discovered that architecture is a perpetual multiplication that never ends since it is woven with a subtle needle sewing water, light, and shadow with memory."[21]

Water, light, and shadow, then, remind us of the gardens of the Alhambra—moving and fascinating elements in which the "Spanish Katsura" also matches the Japanese version. But for the discussion at hand they are a seductive diversion, no less so for the Spanish architects considering the Alhambra in 1952. The reflecting pools would seduce them as much as they seduced Barragán, who would return to them throughout his career: "From one space to the next one goes, from one discovery to the next, as in the courtyards of the Alhambra, so influential upon me."[22]

Last but not least, a significant idea that allows us to understand the powerful appeal of the Alhambra and its vitalizing effect comes from architectural historian G. E. Kidder Smith's sound intuition that there were two "Spains," stumbling upon the first outcome of what we might call the

8 Yasuhiro Ishimoto, photograph of carriage stop, Katsura Imperial Villa.
From *Katsura: Tradition and Creation in Japanese Architecture.*

Steppingstones from the Imperial Carriage Stop to the Gepparo (Moon-Wave Pavilion)

THE ALHAMBRA PALACE, KATSURA OF THE WEST

"spirit of the Alhambra" at the beginning of the 1960s.[23] He discerned a balance between two contradictory forces, what he called the "endemic contrasting tensions in Spain," that he would iconically identify in the opposition between Gaudi's more sensual shapes and the minimalist essence of Ibiza's architecture, and that became one in the Alhambra. It is frequently portrayed as the zenith of Hispano-Arabic architecture: "The Alhambra palace represents the culminating point of seven centuries of culture."[24] Africa and Europe coexist within its walls with an intensity that is unlikely to be found anywhere else in the world—an extraordinary combination of sense and sensibility.

This is the strength of the Alhambra, and will continue to be its strength. In an interview in the 1970s, Barragán asserted: "The Arab palaces may be five or six hundred years old, but their architecture has no epoch; it cannot be classified, it cannot be labeled. That interests me greatly, the idea that architecture loses its epoch in order to allow you to live; it does not locate you or encase you, it does not confine you to the time you are living in. You can also live the past, and along with these two times you can also live the future."[25]

Thus, the soul of the Alhambra was fully present at the beginning of the Spain's architectural rebirth in the twentieth century, when the country recuparated its plenitude of Hispano-Arabic architecture. The *Manifesto of the Alhambra* was, therefore, only the written statement of a vitally critical attitude. That is why it should be compulsory for an architect to visit the Alhambra (or Katsura, if it is closer), but he or she should do it alone and slowly, "without the clumsy steps of the agressive touristic masses that want to watch everything but end up seeing nothing."[26] Only then could the architect repeat the experience Barragán recalled in his 1980 Pritzker Prize acceptance speech when he explained:

> The unexpected discovery of these "jewels" gave me a sensation similar to the one experienced when, having walked through a dark and narrow tunnel of the Alhambra, I suddenly emerged into the serene, silent and solitary "Patio of the Myrtles" hidden in the entrails of that ancient palace. Somehow I had the feeling that it enclosed what a perfect garden no matter its size should enclose: nothing less than the entire Universe. This memorable epiphany has always been with me, and it is not by mere chance that from the first garden for which I am responsible all those following are attempts to capture the echo of the immense lesson to be derived from the aesthetic wisdom of the Spanish Moors.[27]

This lesson has borne much fruit throughout the twentieth century, within Spain and beyond its borders, and continues to reverberate in successive generations of young architects. It should not be lost to the noise, the rush, or the eagerness for fame that agitates modern architectural creation, or, as Walter Gropius had warned, to "vanity, *nouveauté*, and deceit."

Unless otherwise indicated, English translations are by the author.

1   Carlos Jiménez, "Recintos de agua, luz y sombra: Reflexiones sobre la Alhambra," in Ángel Isac, ed., *El manifiesto de la Alhambra: 50 años después : El monumento y la arquitectura contempráneal,* Monografías de la Alhambra 01 (Granada, Spain: Patronato de la Alhambra y Generalife, 2006), 238-247.

2   Hermann Bahr, "El Goethe total," in *Expresionismo* (Murcia: Ed. Galería-librería Yerba, 1998), 111-27. Bahr's book was originally published in German as *Expressionismus* (Munich: Delphin Verlag, 1919).

3   Walter Gropius, postcard to Le Corbusier (June 1954), reprinted in Francesco Dal Co, "La princesse est modeste," in Arata Isozaki, et al., *Katsura: Imperial Villa* (Milan: Electa, 2005), 386.

4   See Mark Wigley, "The Myth of the Local," in Craig Buckley and Pollyanna Rhee, eds., *Architects' Journeys* (New York and Pamplona: GSAPP Books and T6 Ediciones, 2011), 233.

5   José Manuel Pozo, "Arquitectura entre el este y el oeste: A propósito de la abstracción moderna europea,"*Revista RA* 13 (June 2011): 109-22.

6   Fernando Chueca Goitia, *Manifiesto de la Alhambra* (Madrid: Dirección General de Arquitectura, Ministerio de la Gobernación, 1953). While the Manifesto is portrayed as a group effort, Fernando Chueca Goitia was in reality the author of the final document. Attention must be paid to the "Critical Sessions," meetings during which the production of the manifesto was discussed. Many of those present disagreed with the writing of it, but many other contemporary architects that did not attend shared the architectural values represented by the Alhambra. A recent example is the architect José Luis López Zanón, who has attributed decisions in his design for the Universidad Laboral de Cáceres, citing his "fondness for scarcely illuminated spaces leading into other spaces with abundant light, which is the old theme of the Alhambra." This remark was made at a conference held at Escuela de Arquitectura, Universidad de Navarra in November 2012.

7   Chueca, *Manifiesto de la Alhambra*, 5.

8   The Critical Sessions were discussion meetings promoted by Carlos de Miguel, who assembled the most outstanding architects of the time to debate issues pertaining to the progress of the discipline of architecture, usually starting with the critique of a recently constructed building. The debates were later published in the national architecture magazine, *Revista Nacional de Arquitectura*.

9   Juan Miguel Hernández León, "El Manifiesto de la Alhambra," in Isac ed., *El manifiesto de la Alhambra: 50 años después*, 181-85.

10   Wilhelm Worringer, *Abstraktion und Einfühlung* (Munich: Piper & Co. Verlag, 1908). The first Spanish-language edition was *Abstracción y naturaleza* (Mexico: Ed. Fondo de Cultura Económica, 1953).

11   Chueca, *Manifiesto de la Alhambra*, 24.

12   Chueca, *Manifiesto de la Alhambra*, 24.

13   See Louis Kahn, "Monumentality," in Paul Zucker, ed., *New Architecture and City Planning: A Symposium* (Freeport, N.Y.: Books for Libraries Press, 1944), 577-88.

14   See Juan Calatrava, "La Alhambra y el

orientalismo arquitectónico," in *El manifiesto de la Alhambra: 50 años después*, 12–69.

15   Chueca, *Manifiesto de la Alhambra*, 24.

16   Luis Barragán, Pritzker Prize acceptance speech (Dumbarton Oaks, 3 June 1980); reprinted in *Luis Barragán, escritos y conversaciones* (Madrid: El Croquis, 2000), 60.

17   Chueca, *Manifiesto de la Alhambra*, 17.

18   Ibid., 14.

19   Ibid., 14.

20   Walter Gropius, "Architecture in Japan," in *Katsura: Tradition and Creation in Japanese Architecture* (New Haven, CT: Yale University Press, 1960), 8.

21   Jiménez, "Recintos de agua, luz y sombra," 24–41.

22   Luis Barragán, "La Buena Arquitectura es bella," interview by Marie-Pierre Toll (1981), reprinted in *Luis Barragán, escritos y conversaciones*, 132–34.

23   G. E. Kidder Smith, "Spain and Portugal," in *The New Architecture of Europe* (Cleveland and New York: Meridian Books, 1961), 278–89.

24   Rafael Contreras, *Estudio descriptivo de los monumentos árabes de Granada, Sevilla y Córdoba* (1878), cited in Juan Calatrava, "La Alhambra y el orientalismo arquitectónico," 54.

25   Luis Barragán, interview by Elena Poniatowska (November–December, 1976), reprinted in *Luis Barragán, escritos y conversaciones*, 110.

26   Jiménez, "Recintos de agua, luz y sombra," 239.

27   Barragán, Pritzker Prize acceptance speech, 60.

THE LAST MANIFESTO

THE PERMANENCE OF HUMANITY AND THE EPHEMERALITY OF GENIUSES

CARLOS LABARTA & JORGE TÁRRAGO

DURING THE 1980S, a text that had endured the onslaught of postmodernism circulated in Spain's architecture schools in the form of posters and leaflets, successfully fulfilling its aim of becoming a bridge between tradition and modernity. Its author, José Antonio Coderch, near the end of his life could hardly explain how his text, written forty years earlier during the placid month of August 1961, continued to be a key reference point for a new generation of students. Very few people even knew its origin. If the text, *No son genios lo que necesitamos ahora (It Is Not Geniuses We Need Now)*, had the effect of a manifesto, it was not in fact written as one, but was motivated by the author's desire to externalize his deep and intimate thoughts—the textual representation of a working method.

The influence Coderch had on young architects of different generations began at the Barcelona School of Architecture where his text, personality, and work turned the architect into a master as well as an idol. Students, according to recollections by Oscar Tusquets, praised him and attempted to imitate him. Not only did the text became their "bible," but they would also wear the same Clarks shoes, smoke the same Three Nuns tobacco in Peterson pipes (considering them a design wonder), provide illumination for themselves (albeit barely) with his famous wood lamp, and even attempt to design like him (1).[1] Others, like Enric Soria, later would look back and recognize: "The article meant for me a beneficial casting of the experience and personality of that understandable architecture, of simple intentions, bright and precise."[2]

1 José Antonio Coderch smoking a pipe (1981).

LABARTA & TÁRRAGO

Spain was then a country unfamiliar with architectural manifestos; two had been written during the previous decade but their influence was hardly noticeable. The first was written by Luis Moya under the title "Tradicionalistas, funcionalistas y otros" (Traditionalists, Functionalists, and Others), while the second, *Manifiesto de la Alhambra* (the *Manifesto of the Alhambra*), came out of the meeting held by a group of Spanish architects in October 1952 in Granada coordinated by architect Fernando Chueca.[3] Both texts captured the renewal of Spanish architecture that opened the way to modernity without rejecting tradition—in the first case focusing on composition features, and in the second case on the search of common elements from modernity and Spanish tradition. These openings toward modernity were also the outcome of tentative encounters with architecture abroad, including Chueca's direct knowledge of American reality from his stay in New York between 1951 and 1952.[4]

The *Manifesto of the Alhambra* was signed by twenty-four architects, but did not include Coderch. The previous year, in August 1951, he had founded the Grupo R at his own office.[5] His purpose was also to stimulate a debate on international architecture that would open up Catalan architecture to modernity. Although the group was continuously active for ten years, Coderch abandoned it in 1953, moving away from its manifesto and slogans to elaborate a more introspective reflection founded on his personal experience and ethical position.

Coderch had been the first Spanish architect to reach international attention as a result of the interest that his first works aroused in Gio Ponti

2 José Antonio Coderch, Spanish Pavilion, Milán Triennale (1951).

THE LAST MANIFESTO

who, after visiting Barcelona in April 1949, published Coderch's work in the pages of *Domus* and invited him to organize the Spanish Pavilion at the Milan Triennale in 1951 (2).[6] This international acknowledgment consolidated when Josep Lluís Sert proposed that Coderch participate in the CIAM meeting in Otterlo in 1959, where he would present the project for the Hotel and Apartments at Torre Valentina (3).[7] That meeting was dominated by the struggle between the rhetoric of written discourse and built work, eventually leaning towards building—which undoubtedly satisfied Coderch's interests and turned him into one of the actual victors of the congress, although he would not likely have considered himself in these terms. In fact, in a letter sent to Dutch architect Jaap Bakema he recognized how extremely useful the Otterlo meetings had been for him. It is not in vain that the aim of the congress, as set down in the letter of invitation, was "to determine if a true affinity of thought exists between participants not only in spoken and written words but, more profoundly, at the level of plastic invention through the communication of direct building ideas."[8]

At the congress, each architect was asked to present his work and propose a written explanation of his interests. The most professional and brief of all explanations collected in the minutes belongs to Coderch. His essay contains not a single conceptual justification or theoretical positioning; only his programmatic, landscaping, and constructive solutions are clearly stated.

It is an eminently pragmatic essay. This approach was common to other participants and did not go unnoticed by Louis Kahn, who spoke of

3 José Antonio Coderch presenting his project for Torre Valentina, Otterlo (1959).

a need to transcend simple pragmatics in his closing speech: "I have had the good fortune to observe the plans and work of men here, and have seen that almost everyone started with the solution of the problem, given the conditions upon which design was made. But I think I may say freely that very few started with a kind of sense of realization of the problem and then inserted design as its natural extension—a circumstantial thing, because I really do believe that design is a circumstantial thing."[9]

The interest in the development of humankind's habitat, and not only for the evolution of modern architecture, provoked the end of CIAM at Otterlo, which also became the starting point of a new center for the exchange of ideas and experiences: the Post Box for Habitat Development, (B.P.H.).[10] Coordinated by Bakema, the B.P.H. facilitated the communication between architects such as the Smithsons, Ralph Erskine, Cornelis Van Eesteren, Jerzy Soltan, and others, and resulted in the dissolution of the programmatic, collective manifesto in favor of a more individual exchange of ideas (a sort of modern-era Dropbox where information could be exchanged). Between September 1959 and July 1971, when Bakema announced the B.P.H.'s dissolution, eighteen themes, concerning the improvement of the built environment, prompted exchanges between architects.[11] As presented on the cover of the September 1959 issue of the magazine *Forum*—whose editorial board included Bakema and Aldo van Eyck—the topics and concepts of debate related to issues such as identity, visual groupings, devices of identification, harmony in motion, the habitat for the majority of people, mobility, hierarchy of human associations, corridor space, imagination versus common sense, change and growth, and the architectural principle of the cluster.

In May 1960, Coderch sent a proposal for consideration in a following meeting, confirming his interest in the moral position of architecture: "What for me is essential is the ethical position of architecture in front of the problems of our time. I am interested in knowing the architect and his reasons in all the works that seem relevant to me."[12] The collective manifesto lost its interest and personal commitment became the best way of expressing the individual link with the evolution of architecture beyond doctrine.

Coderch hardly wrote. He "wrote" with his buildings and projects, rather than develop theories about them. At the beginning of the 1960s, coinciding with the changes occurring in the publishing of manifestos, Coderch wrote the most important of his scarce writings. As a consequence of the aforementioned international connections he was invited to participate in Team Ten. On the occasion of his admission he sent Bakema a statement of principles through B.P.H entitled "It Is Not Geniuses We Need

Now."[13] (4) Undoubtedly moved by the text, Bakema responded by sending him an inscribed copy of *Le petit prince* by Antoine de Saint-Exupéry.

Coderch's text reflects his deeply personal thinking, countering speculation with individual experimentation. It is, at the same time, the result of an elaborated process of distillation. Numerous previous drafts preceded its final publication, a process of refinement comparable to Coderch's architecture, inseparable from the coherence and rigor of his calculated words.[14]

The value of experimentation, and of diligence before speculation, is summed up by the architect as follows: "To bring this about I believe that we must first rid ourselves of many ideas that appear clear but are false, of many hollow words, and work, each and every one of us, with that good will

4 José Antonio Coderch, "It Is Not Geniuses We Need Now,"
original typescript sent to Bakema (August 1961).

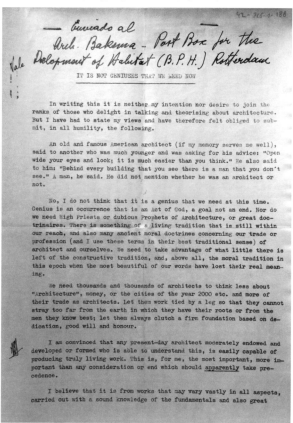

that is translated into one's own work and teaching rather than with a mere concentration on doctrinarism."[15]

The original essay—held in the CIAM archives at the ETH in Zurich—consists of five typewritten and hand-corrected pages, each initialed in the right margin as if it were a will. It is an unmistakable sign of the value assigned by the architect and the personal identification with its content. The manifesto is substituted by a commitment. The word is placed face to face with the work in complete coherence, as if to dilute the distance between intellect and perception.

The most singular phrase of the text weighs the need for a collective architectural craft to serve humankind's needs against the singularity

5 José Antonio Coderch, "It Is Not Geniuses We Need Now," original typescript sent to Jaap Bakema with handwritten addendum (August 1961).

of a genius: "No, I do not think that it is a genius that we need at this time. Genius is an occurrence that is an Act of God, a goal, not an end. Nor do we need High Priests or dubious Prophets of Architecture, or great doctrinaires."[16] (This "Act of God" in the original text claims a moral position that was eliminated explicitly from the later revision, even while it underlies the whole text.)

The architect, more used to building than writing, could not hold back the temptation of referring to his most recent design. In a handwritten addendum to the typescript sent to Bakema, he describes his happiness at having met Gropius, and adds: "As soon as it is ready I will send you the new lamp I have drawn with several difficulties. Its aspect is very similar to the one you own. I will try to make the leaves really white."[17] (5)

The text was not initially conceived for publication. However, both the original and the subsequent versions were published in different languages and countries, during the turbulent 1960s, when Spanish architecture started to be noticed abroad. The text was first published in *Domus* in November 1961 and in the Portuguese magazine *Arquitectura* in December 1961, appearing later in *L'architecture d'aujourd'hui* in February–March, 1962, and then in *Architectural Design* in December 1962.[18]

Coderch's works were reproduced alongside the text. (6, 7) It was this independent, foreign verification of the honest quality of that architecture that triggered the publication of his essay. A subtle difference of meaning appears in the translation of the title into French: "Architecture pour l'homme ou architecture géniale," which contrasts extraordinary architecture with architecture for man, as if genius were not compatible with the service our profession must provide. However, what is truly brilliant in architecture is found in the efficient resolution of problems, something that a good friend of Coderch, Javier Carvajal, made crystal clear: "Architecture is an art with need-solving reasons."[19] Coderch's essay was the first text by a Spanish architect published in *L'architecture d'aujourd'hui*. Its influence was decisive not only in the evolution of Coderch's career but in Spanish architecture as a whole. Following an editorial decision, a project by Mies van der Rohe—the headquarters for Krupp industries in Essen, Germany—was published on the opposite page. The Spanish architect achieved international recognition next to one of the masters of modern architecture.

Coderch's built works had already been published in Portugal.[20] But the Portuguese publication of his text in *Arquitectura*, which preceded the French publication, would also prove relevant to the essay's reception, as it would coincide with a similar context of debate between modernity and tradition taking place in Portuguese architecture.

The journal *Architectural Design*, edited by Monica Pidgeon and Kenneth Frampton, published Alison Smithson's *Team 10 Primer* in 1962. This was a document that gathered the articles, essays, and diagrams which the group regarded as central to their individual positions, and Coderch's essay received accolades from his Team Ten colleagues. Perhaps the most moving among them came from Eduard Sekler who conveyed his happiness to Coderch in a letter retained in Coderch's archives (8).[21]

In 1991, during an interview in which Aldo van Eyck recalled his memories of different members of Team Ten, he would note: "What should I say about Antonio Coderch? Except that he was the most gifted architect of the lot. A great architect. He was very emotional, he didn't argue much, a solitary figure; he was severe, morally severe, but not dogmatic; he was a puritan and catholic. He was a genius architect. He wrote the article 'It Is Not Geniuses We Need Now' but he really was a genius, a fantastic architect, an artist. He was a highly complicated person, a modernist in terms of architecture, a great lover of Miró and Lorca and a great friend of them too; on the other hand, he was from a sort of basic Catalan aristocrat family."[22]

In short, Coderch's text transcends the author and acquires a universal value, as a proposal spread over an international reality but at the same time springing from a clear local conscience. Against the short life span of certain manifestos, Coderch's text has lasted over time, which allows for a

6 José Antonio Coderch, Casa Ugalde, Caldes d´Estrac (1951).

THE LAST MANIFESTO

number of interpretations, just like good architecture. The manifesto can thus be understood as a single document that endures and allows for being adapted according to circumstances. Since its aim is not to impress but to be led by an attitude of social service, its teachings still remain valid.

The most important variations to its structure occurred when Coderch decided to use the same text for his admission speech to the Royal Fine Arts Academy of San Jorge in Barcelona, in 1977, with the title "Espiritualidad de la Arquitectura" (9). Using the same basic structure for the essay—evidence that his convictions were firm—here he points out five distinct categories: unnecessary geniuses, ideas and words, hateful materialism, the spiritual quality of the architect, and problems influencing architecture. His ethical commitment to architecture is reassured with the inclusion of two new references toward the end of the text. The first is to Goethe and concerns the conflict between faith and skepticism. The second one refers to a quotation from Einstein that Coderch kept in his office:

7 José Antonio Coderch, Apartments in Barceloneta, Barcelona (1951).

"The most beautiful thing that a man can feel is the mysterious side of life. There lies the cradle of true Art and Science."[23]

The afterlife of the text did not end at that point. Thirty-five years after its initial publication, in 1996, Peter Smithson reflected on the original writings. He and Coderch had met at the 1959 CIAM in Otterlo, exchanged correspondence, and the echoes of the words and buildings of the Catalan architect reverberated in Smithson's memories. "My first knowledge of this statement came from Alison's publication of it as Coderch's contribution to the original version of the *Team 10 Primer*, in *Architectural Design*, December 1962."[24]

Peter Smithson was far more moved by Coderch's work than by the words of his manifesto. (10) "Of course one has to be careful with words, they adumbrate, often falsely, the thoughts, or more critically, the

8 Eduard Sekler, letter to José Antonio Coderch (November 1961).

posture of the speaker. But buildings... think of Mies' Farnsworth House, Le Corbusier's Armé de Salut, Duiker's Zonnerstraal, Kahn's Trenton Bath House. Words may have helped (I doubt it), but it is the building that it is the ethic."[25] Going further into the sense of ethics, Smithson points out: "The ethic of Coderch is in its formal and organizational persistence, in its devotion to the act of dwelling, to a possibly perfectible domesticity."[26] This leads us to consider the distance between the expectations generated by the words in manifestos and the built work deriving from them. Coderch's essay is one of the few in which that difference barely exists. Perhaps this is because, as has been pointed out, his writings are essentially pragmatic: his is not a theoretical text, but a code of conduct.

The manifesto can be understood as a revolutionary wager or, as is in the case of Coderch, a continuity or revisionist writing that finds in its precedents the evocation for new formulations. As Coderch affirms in his text: "There is something of a living tradition that is still within our reach, and also many ancient moral doctrines concerning our trade or profession (and I use these terms in their best traditional sense) of architect and ourselves. We need to take advantage of what little there is left of the constructive tradition, and, above all, the moral tradition in this epoch when the most beautiful of our words have lost their real meaning."[27]

103

9 José Antonio Coderch, speech upon his admission to the Royal Fine Arts Academy of San Jorge in Barcelona (1977).

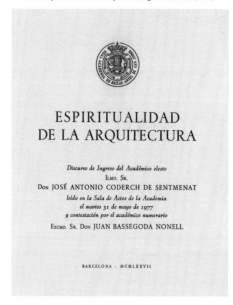

ESPIRITUALIDAD DE LA ARQUITECTURA

Discurso de Ingreso del Académico electo
Ilmo. Sr.
Don JOSÉ ANTONIO CODERCH DE SENTMENAT
leído en la Sala de Actos de la Academia
el martes 31 de mayo de 1977
y contestación por el académico numerario
Excmo. Sr. Don JUAN BASSEGODA NONELL

BARCELONA · MCMLXXVII

LABARTA & TÁRRAGO

While invoking tradition, Coderch synthesizes critical and professional authority and alerts us to the impossibility of an effective manifesto if both worlds become divided. The architect Enric Soria looked back on Coderch's essay decades later: "At that time J. A. Coderch's professional authority was unquestionable. His independence and reserve concerning the most dynamic centers of the new architectural culture, at odds with the political situation of the moment, turned his rare appearances into anticipated, relevant, and erudite messages."[28] Wisdom and cultivation did not only coexist with the professional world, they were the only medium in which Coderch found his true identity.

At our present moment of mobility and relativism, how can we develop manifestos concerning stability and security if ours is a time of mutations and multiplicities? The manifesto as an evident and heroic expression of found truths has been substituted by the formulation of aspirations and wishes. The word *manifesto*, almost by definition, means a dogmatic and revolutionary essay—which runs counter to our present sensibilities.

10 José Antonio Coderch, Apartments in Barceloneta, Barcelona (1951), interior view.

THE LAST MANIFESTO

Thus, the answer to the question of what has happened to architectural manifestos is directly related to the loss of faith in architecture. As the Spanish architect Luis Fernández-Galiano recently asked, "What happens when we lose faith in architecture itself, when we perceive it in the end as no more than a gentlemanly sport for educated minds and well-trained eyes?"[29] For him modern architecture offered us a credo, a credo we lost faith in forty years ago.

This might not be a time for manifestos, nor for an excess of words, nor vanities, but rather a time for understanding the profession as a service in which architecture and its inhabitants become the true leading characters. As stated by Coderch himself, "Of course, it is clear that this means accepting our own limitations."[30]

In "It Is Not Geniuses We Need Now" the word *manifesto* is only used to critique a certain attitude: "There is an architect here who, shortly after leaving his school of architecture, published a form or manifesto on costly paper, after having designed a chair, if it can be called such."[31] This implicit critique shows Coderch's skeptical attitude toward the genre of the manifesto. Undoubtedly Coderch preferred facts to theories.

Contemporary society is saturated with information and can only be moved by facts. Consequently, rather than a time of manifestos, ours is a time of evocations. In that spirit, we might examine a photograph of Coderch's work by the photographer Francesc Català-Roca, who documented many of Coderch's buildings and was able to create new realities from the

11 Francesc Català-Roca, Almodovar del Pinar, Cuenca, Spain, (1954).

architect's work. (11) At first glance reality hides what shadows display, a result of the effect of light. In other words, what reality hides is shown by shadows. Architects have the duty to create works that can enlighten reality, transform it, so that humankind may be able to perceive all that reality itself does not portray. Therefore, as a spotlight on reality, architecture may be acknowledged without the need of being obvious.

Manifestos then clearly become no longer a collection of irrefutable truths, but rather the wise construction of those artifacts sheltering the needs and desires of human beings. Coderch's essay did not pretend to be a manifesto, but it has in fact become the final manifesto and its echoes are still valid. Coderch's simple words, paradoxically, make up Spanish architecture's last manifesto.

To conclude, we offer one of the teachings that Coderch repeated to his students, perhaps even evoking a well-known photograph of his colleague Shadrach Woods. (12) "Don't try to intellectualize your creative act too much: it is much easier to learn how to ride a bicycle than to understand the physical principles behind it."[32] Time to pedal.

12 Shadrach Woods riding a bicycle in Paris.

THE LAST MANIFESTO

1   Oscar Tusquets, "Recuerdos de un grandísimo arquitecto," *El País/Quadern* (May 2000), archived online at http://www.tusquets.com/fichaa/390/recuerdos-de-un-grandiacutesimo-arquitecto, accessed September 14, 2011.

2   Enric Soria, "Comentario," *WAM* (1996), http://www.arranz.net/web.arch-mag.com/1/recy/recy1p.html, accessed September 14, 2011.

3   Luis Moya, "Tradicionalistas, funcionalistas y otros," in *Revista Nacional de Arquitectura* 150 (1950), 261; and *Manifiesto de la Alhambra* (Dirección General de Arquitectura, Madrid, 1953).

4   As a result of his stays in North America, Chueca published the books *Viviendas de renta reducida en los Estados Unidos* (Madrid: Instituto de Estudios de Administración Local, 1952) and *Nueva York, forma y sociedad* (Madrid: Instituto de Estudios de la Admistración Local, 1953).

5   The Grupo R developed its activities between 1951 and 1961. Among its members, along with Coderch, were the architects Josep Maria Sostres, Antoni de Moragas, Joaquim Gili, and Manuel Valls, as well as young architects including Oriol Bohigas, Josep Martorell, and Manuel Ribas i Piera. See Carme Rodriguez, *Grup R* (Barcelona: Gustavo Gili, 1994).

6   The first international publication of Coderch's work is presented under the title "Due ville a Sitges: Garriga Nogués-Las Forcas-Casa Compte," in *Domus* 240 (November 1949).

7   The list of attendees was prepared by the coordinating group led by Bakema. The architects were invited as individuals without representing any geographical, political, or religious tendency or ideology.

8   Oscar Newman, *CIAM '59 in Otterlo* (Stuttgart: Karl Krämer Verlag, 1961), 7.

9   Louis Kahn, "Talk at the Conclusion of the Otterlo Congress," in Newman, *CIAM '59 in Otterlo*, 205.

10   The capital initial letters B.P.H. were common to all three languages used for the group's communiqués—English, French, and German: Post Box for Habitat Development (B.P.H.), Boîte Postale pour le développement de l´Habitat (B.P.H.) , and Briefkasten für die Entwicklung von Habitat (B.P.H.)

11   The dissolution was announced by Bakema in a letter: "Dear Colleagues, since 1959 I maintained some contact among some people, who struggled for a better human built environment, by the BPH-letters. This is the last one made in the Posthoornstraat 12b, as was promised at the CIAM. Otterlo 1959 conference. From now communications of this kind will be done by means of Carré Bleu, where André Schimmerling will take over, as was decided at Team X meeting 1971." Jaap Bakema, letter to B.P.H. participants, Institut für Geschichte und Theorie der Architektur Archiv, ETH-Zurich, (August, 11, 1971); archive hereafter abbreviated as GTA.

12   José Antonio Coderch, text sent to the Post Box for Habitat Development (B.P.H.), GTA (May 29, 1960).

13   José Antonio Coderch, "It Is Not Geniuses We Need Now," original text sent to Bakema on the occasion of Coderch's admission to Team 10, GTA (August 1961).

14   Coderch's working process was explained to the authors in an interview with José Antonio Coderch Giménez, architect and son of José Antonio Coderch (October 6, 2011). There is an echo of Mies in Coderch's words: "I do not oppose form, but only form as a goal. And I do this as the result of a number of experiences and the insight I have gained from them. Ludwig Mies van der Rohe, "On Form in Architecture," in Ulrich Conrads, *Programs and Manifestoes on 20th-Century Architecture* (Cambridge, MA: The MIT Press, 1970), 102.

15   Coderch. "It Is Not Geniuses We Need Now," 2.

16   Coderch, "It Is Not Geniuses We Need Now," 1.

17   Coderch, handwritten addition to "It Is Not Geniuses We Need Now," 5. Translation by the authors.

18   José Antonio Coderch, "Architecture pour l'homme ou architecture géniale," *L'architecture d'aujourd'hui*, 100 (February–March 1962). Originally published in the Italian magazine *Domus* 384 (November 1961), as "Non é di genii che abbiamo bisogno," it also appeared in the Portuguese magazine *Arquitectura* 73 (December 1961), and in *Architectural Design* 32, no. 12 (December, 1962). The text was translated into other languages; for example a Japanese version was included some years later in a special issue devoted to José Antonio Coderch, *A+U* 62 (February 1976).

19   This sentence is part of the oral tradition and was constantly repeated by Javier Carvajal to his students. See Javier Carvajal, *Curso abierto, lecciones de arquitectura para arquitectos y no arquitectos* (Madrid: Servicio de Publicaciones Colegio Oficial de Arquitectos de Madrid, 1997), 43.

20   José Antonio Coderch and Manuel Valls Vergés,, "Habitaçoes em Setges," *Arquitectura portuguesa Ceràmica e Edificaçao, Reunidas* 39 (February 1947): 8–14.

21   Eduard Sekler, letter to José Antonio Coderch, Coderch Archive (November 15, 1961). "Dear Coderch, your excellent essay was forwarded to me from Vienna and I must say I was not only impressed by it: it made me feel happy! Because it showed to me that I am not alone with a way of thinking in a materialistic world. You have expressed well some sentiments which could have been my own. [Jerzy] Soltan happens to be here this year, as a visiting critic, and I sent your paper to him. He also liked it very much and we are going to have a discussion about it. I very much hope to see you one of these days and to talk with you. In the meantime all good wishes for your further work and a cordial handshake. As ever yours, Eduard F. Sekler. P.S. I also talked to Sert about your paper which he liked very much!"

22   Aldo van Eyck, interview with Clelia Tuscano (September 26, 1991) entitled "On Team 10," in *Aldo van Eyck Writings: Collected Articles and Other Writings 1947-1998* (Amsterdam: SUN Publishers, 2008), 610–21.

23   José Antonio Coderch, *Espiritualidad de la arquitectura* (Barcelona: Real Academia de Bellas Artes de San Jorge, 1977), 12. Published as the entrance lecture given on May 31, 1977.

24   Peter Smithson, "Comment," *WAM* (1996), http://www.arranz.net/web.arch-mag.com/1/recy/recy1p.html, accessed September 14, 2011.

25   Smithson, "Comment."

26   Smithson, "Comment."

27   Coderch, "It Is Not Geniuses We Need Now," 1.

28   Soria, "Comentario."

29   Luis Fernández-Galiano, "Losing Faith in Architecture", *Harvard Design Magazine* (Fall 2007/Winter 2008): 53.

30   Coderch, "It Is Not Geniuses We Need Now," 3.

31   Coderch, "It Is Not Geniuses We Need Now," 3.

32   José Antonio Coderch, as quoted in Tusquets, "Recuerdos de un grandísimo arquitecto."

108

THE LAST MANIFESTO

CONTEMPORARY ARCHITECTURE AND THE MANIFESTO GENRE

JUAN M. OTXOTORENA

THE AIM OF THIS ESSAY is to contribute to the debate on the relevance of the manifesto in contemporary architecture.[1] Underlying this debate is a question: What is the state of the manifesto in the current culture of architecture? In a sense the manifesto is an artifact of the past, its form associated with the Modern Movement and polemical practices that arose in its wake. Ulrich Conrads's anthology *Programs and Manifestoes on 20th-Century Architecture* (1964, German; and 1970, English), for instance, was already laden with an air of nostalgia; it sought to mark a before and after and open a new chapter for the manifesto.[2] The book had identified the demise of a literary genre that had intensely considered the "obligations of architecture" to society and to the discipline itself. The manifesto was rhetorically *de rigueur* for the avant-garde of the early twentieth century; it was widely cultivated in speeches and propaganda from Leninists to Dadaists. But the form has fallen out of fashion. What follows sketches out some possible explanations.

The first, and most obvious, is the spectacular change of cultural circumstances. Historical conditions might not be more demanding or complex than they were in the past, but the societal relationship to history has changed. The voice of the avant-garde has lost its vigor; the future is no longer a territory to be conquered but rather a site of trepedation, or worse, disinterest. Today's scholarship debates the consequences of "The End of History."[3] And while our era still has produced movements that voice collective claims, the tone has changed.

Shifting attitudes in Spanish architecture reflect these larger forces of cultural change. In the decades preceding the 1950s, Spanish architects strove to assert their cutting-edge sensibilities and vociferously supported the Modern Movement. They were countering a public perception anchored in nostalgic notions of tradition and the picturesque, with entrenched tastes bordering on kitsch. After this period, however, little more than lip service was paid to the defense of architecture as a cultural and artistic discipline.

During the 1930s, vibrant, spirited manifestos favoring the new architecture in Spain abounded. The empassioned exhortations of the Grupo de Artistas y Técnicos Españoles para la Arquitectura Contem-poránea (GATEPAC) were undoubtedly significant in the years just before the Spanish Civil War (1936–39).[4] They demonstate a strong combination of optimism, faith, and energy. Twenty years later, there appeared the ambitious debates around the famous *Manifiesto de la Alhambra* (1953),[5] led by the architect and scholar Fernando Chueca; on Luis Moya's critical positions against modernity in the main architectural magazine of the country at the time, *Revista Nacional de Arquitectura,*[6] or about the founding ideology of Grupo R (R Group) in Catalonia.[7] However, things would change drastically in the ensuing decades.

The 1960s marked a turning point in architectural rhetoric. The Modern Movement was undergoing disciplinary critique. Meanwhile, in Spain, the profession had found solid economic footing. There was plenty of work for a new generation of well-prepared architects; the interaction between architecture and the arts was becoming stronger (as Chillida and Oteiza's work shows); new architecture schools were emerging (in Seville, Valencia, Navarra, Valladolid, and Coruña among other places); and intellectual debate was taking root. Practitioners were making statements, not leveling theoretical claims. Yet, production and pragmatism prevailed over philosophical discussion and the space for the manifesto was shrinking.

This shift started with the famous essay written in 1961 by the architect José Antonio Coderch: "No son genios lo que necesitamos ahora" (It is not geniuses that we need now).[8] This essay portrays the mindset of a whole generation, and for more than twenty years dominated discourse. It is a true manifesto. Frequently translated and omnipresent during its time, this manifesto asserts the social mission of the architect. It is singular not because it was an outlier, but because it was unanimously accepted. Until the end of the 1970s it was printed on extra-large sized posters emphatically placed on the doors of architecture schools.

Traces of its zeal are palpable in certain contemporary proclamations denouncing what was seen as a sad decline of the discipline. The proclamations of Esteve Bonell and his team of architects defending the dignity of the profession in 1998 come to mind,[9] or the positions represented by the group Arquitectes per l'Arquitectura (AxA).[10] These groups are motivated by a love of the architectural profession and a strong ethical conviction, backed by the solid accomplishments of their members.

Coderch aside, in the Spanish context it seems there have been hardly any proper manifestos since the 1950s, and none before the "modern revolution." If there are any, they refer only to the unstable future of the architectural profession. Their scarcity has to do with their fatalism. We should take a look at the causes of this.

The phenomenon responds to the increasingly evident difficulties for the survival and "salvation" of the archetype of the traditional Spanish architect: the autonomous, independent, and craft-oriented architect. Legally, the architect had the main role in controlling building processes, and was used to working according to personal standards—technical and ethical—in what was perceived as a craft of ingenuity, inventiveness, and individual responsibility. Changes in capitalism and a market increasingly focused on expendability have marginalized such a traditional profile and altered the value of design. It seems that design increases the product's price and only adds additional energy consumption.

What this produces is not only a romantic way of understanding and organizing the the work of building, which has given rise in part to an image of the architect-as-*prima donna*. It also yields a working that might generate unbearably overbudgeted construction and added management complexity and insecurities. Unsurprisingly, especially in a climate of economic recession, this diminishes the reputuation of the architect in the larger society. This is, at least for the Italian architect Gio Ponti (who participated in events with Grupo R), what underlies Spanish architecture's international recognition, which is certainly endangered.[11]

There was a time for impassioned speeches in favor of the rationality of modern abstraction, but the era of an architecture so concerned with its identity as art and cultural discipline has subsided. The profession faces new questions now, but it has perhaps retained that introverted process of reflection formed in the infancy of modernity.

We have seen two great moments regarding program statements: those related to the campaign favoring the modern movement, and our current claims about the profession. Meanwhile, history has witnessed new stances regarding its "calling" that, although they might sometimes disregard the classical format of the manifesto, invoke its spirit.

The latter includes the ideas of collectives or movements needing to vocalize a radical direction amid the magma of an entropic reality. A similar relationship to the past can be found in the varying "isms" that have been replacing one another in the architectural scene. These have riffed on discourses of the past century to reveal themselves authentically "modern," thus contributing to radical change in the figurative arts and offering alternative modernisms.

The manifesto finds a certain continuity in the vibrating succession of modernism's iterative orthodoxy, which we have been witnessing since before Team Ten's honest opening toward the vernacular.[12] Revisionist stances taken by the so-called Second and Third Generation fall in line,[13] as do alternative ethoses like organicism, the rediscovery of the "space age,"[14] and the new utopia linked to pop culture—visible in the work of groups like Archigram.[15] There is, however, a clear distance between these positions and ambitious modernist pronouncements. They no longer deal with bombastic assertive statements of the new, but rather with a response they generate over time, articulated in terms of rebellion and disobedience.[16]

In the context of postmodernism[17] they become even more radical, their uninhibited turmoil giving rise to new narratives and developing the conceptual axis for possible neo-avant-gardes.[18] Among these are Robert Venturi's *Complexity and Contradiction in Architecture,* including all its anti-establishment sensibility and advocacy for an "architecture parlante" adapted to consumerism; the consolidation of a vaguely neoclassic "tendency" around Aldo Rossi and his famous *L'architettura della città;* and even the linguistic formalism found in the work of the New York Five.[19]

This too, though, is the past. We have reshaped the discourse once again. The catharsis linked to deconstructivism, which views itself as a new beginning with its revolutionary frame for formal experimentation, can also be seen as an end, a means of foreclosing the manifesto's polemical cry.[20] The contradictions of deconstructivism in many ways mark the apex of the last century of architectural thought.

So, the spirit of "isms" has faded, we have exhausted linguistic inspiration; a show business logic and a fascination with the image dominate the evolution of our information and consumer society.[21] This generalization is especially true regarding the crisis of the Spanish professional model. The classical role of what up until now was considered a craft is gasping its last breath. What seems to be succeeding it is an animated rivalry among anonymous brands adapted to the dynamics of commercial strategies, expensive signature design, and "ready-to-wear" standardized offerings. Design now appears subject to a systematic and, perhaps, unconscious processes of cross-pollination and emulation, competing to forge a "new frontier" in our marketing culture. Thus, we face a profession with a crisis, a discipline without aim. The banal and anti-conceptual practices have obtained power and demonstrate no restraint.

However, all is not lost. Today there is also cause for grand statements and optimistic sentiment. We oscillate between ethics and show business, between method and stardom, between systematic and relativistic rigor, between magnanimous service and narcissistic self-contemplation, between hard-working craft and the inhumane alienation of anonymous production, between social idealism and the sad "trash-TV" audience, between mastery and performance, between intense aesthetic demands and vain blazes of showmanship.

Every architect is called to position herself or himself in relation to this dichotomy. Yet, it is critical to pause and assess the two poles and consider their seeming contradictions; and it is prudent to avoid excesses at either end of the pendulum. The language of violent diatribes and agitated gesticulations may be flashy and feel urgent, but in the end it is excessive, unsustainable, and serves no tangible purpose. It will have very little effect on the professional scene. Controversy in fact can lend attention and legitimacy to weak and ill-founded positions. Among other things, there are new arguments to assimilate: as infuriated as we might be by rampant banality or frivolous architecture, we cannot maintain a discourse rigidly bound to the traditional argument of the proportion between means and goals without opening it to an already unavoidable broader horizon.

A conclusion could be as follows:

1.

There is a need to channel the outrage caused by the architectural insanities generated by our society. We are undoubtedly disturbed by the economic crisis we have been suffering since the end of 2008. It has caught us off balance, both experts and laymen, and there are plenty of explanations that might serve to direct our future actions.

It is one thing, however, to channel social outrage—something that is probably necessary but easily subject to changing moods. It is a very different thing to solve the problems behind this outrage. We must measure our words and not let initial perceptions turn into conclusions right away to avoid reactionary analysis and antagonistic logics.

2.

Circumstances call for positions, individually and collectively, as analysts and activists, in the intellectual realm and the professional field. In general terms, we are no longer modern. What this essay suggests is that architecture is about to be substituted by show business style and banal standardization. In this case there would be only one pending manifesto: the one condemning it.

Many would subscribe to an aspiration toward an ethical architecture, committed to the observance of the classical standards of technical rigor, economic rationality, functional efficiency, spatial qualities, and formal reliability (*utilitas*, *firmitas*, and *venustas*). They would vehemently rail against the idea that architecture is merely devoted to showy facades and high-revenue real estate. However, as has been said, one must go beyond the realm of the mere reactive protest.

One should be suspicious of the hand-wringers and doomsayers, the harsh cadence of the close minded. Architects should find their voice in the poetics of conversation; they should embrace questions and critique. These are the things that bolster conviction.

At the same time, we are not free from the temptation to cooperate with the forces battling to drag us toward disaster. Without vigiliance and principles one could end up aligning with the empty ghostly architecture we so deeply scorn. But we must be fair: to a great extent everybody ends up doing the architecture they can. Choice is a bit of a luxury, and there is always someone willing to meet the demand.

3.

The "symbolic manifesto" is currently valid: it warns us, and it has a symptomatic role that we must not disdain.

4.

And, finally, there are the interstices of polarized discourse, the spaces between service and image, or rigor and show business, that push our understanding and call for new methods. Gaudy commercialism and pure form are not as easy to isolate as one would desire in order to renounce them. Efforts to marginalize them run the risk of only further validating their existence.

The drift of modern architecture toward a simple International Style, for example, could not have been more tragic. Its reduction to a mere fashion was defined in terms of language. We cannot forget Mies's famous aphorism: "We refuse to recognize problems of form, but only problems of building. Form is not the aim of our work..."[22] This sort of rejection of shape is always inherently paradoxical.[23]

So in this climate of crisis, a bit of careful consideration could go a long way. There is no time like the present to reflect on the basic principles that undergird the practice of architecture. It is not a matter of keeping the architect from shaping the world; architects will always be compelled by "the obligation to build," as Manfredo Tafuri would say.[24] A look to the past, though, sheds light on the complexity of current circumstances, and may even bring into them the optimism of an earlier era.

1   The validity of the manifesto as a genre in contemporary architecture was the topic of a symposium titled "What Happened to the Architectural Manifesto?" organized in November 2011 by Columbia University in collaboration with the University of Navarra School of Architecture at Columbia University Graduate School of Architecture, Planning and Preservation.

2   See Ulrich Conrads, *Programs and Manifestoes on 20th-Century Architecture* (Cambridge, MA: The MIT Press, 1970).

3   See Francis Fukayama, *The End of History and the Last Man* (New York: Free Press, 1992), and *The Great Disruption: Human Nature and the Reconstitution of Social Order* (New York: Free Press, 1999), or even Samuel P. Huntington, "The Clash of Civilizations?," *Foreign Affairs,* vol. 72, no. 3 (Summer 1993): 22–49. Also see Alba A. Fernández, *Los axiomas del crepúsculo: Ética y estética de la arquitectura,* Serie Arte, Perspectivas (Madrid: Hermann Blume, 1990).

4   See, for example, José Manuel Aizpurúa, "Cuándo habrá arquitectura?," *La Gaceta Literaria,* March 1, 1930, as well as the complete collection of consecutive issues of *AC* magazine compiled as facsimile in Francesc Roca Rossell, ed., *AC GATEPAC 1931–1937* (Barcelona: Gustavo Gili, 1975).

5   On this subject see Fernando Chueca Goitia, *Invariantes castizos de la arquitectura española; Invariantes de la arquitectura hispanoamericana; Manifiesto de la Alhambra* (Madrid: DOSSAT, 1979). In 1950, backed by *Arquitectura,* the magazine of Madrid's official architects' association (Colegio de Arquitectos de Madrid) a group of achitects started meeting periodically to discuss the situation of their profession though the analysis of the most relevant buildings in Spanish architectural history. The discussion turned toward the "modern and contemporary" value of a building that had begun construction in the thirteenth century: the Alhambra in Granada. Two years after starting these sessions, the architects decided to visit Granada and hold their debates at the Alhambra to discuss the building itself. When the October 1952 meeting ended, Fernando Chueca Goitia summarized all of his notes and wrote a document that would become known as the *Manifiesto de la Alhambra,* a long text that stated among its conclusions that the Alhambra constituted an "essential reservoir for modern architecture." Also see *Manifiesto de la Alhambra,* with a prologue by Fernando Chueca Goitia, preliminary studies by Ángel Isac, and coda by Emilio de Santiago Simón (Granada, Spain: Fundación Rodríguez-Acosta/Delegación en Granada del Colegio Oficial de Arquitectos de Andalucía Oriental, 1993) and Ángel Isac, ed., *El Manifiesto de la Alhambra 50 años después: El monumento y la arquitectura contemporánea/The Alhambra Manifesto 50 Years Later: The Monument and Contemporary Architecture,* Monografías de la Alhambra 01, (Granada, Spain: Patronato de la Alhambra y el Generalife, 2006).

6   See Luis Moya, "Tradicionalistas, funcionalistas y otros" (I and II), *Revista Nacional de Arquitectura* 102 and 103, 1960.

7   See Centro de Cultura Contemporánea de Barcelona, *Grupo R: Una revisión de la modernidad 1951–1961* (Barcelona: Centro de Cultura Contemporánea de Barcelona/Institut d'Edicions de la Diputació de Barcelona, 1997).

8   José Antonio Coderch's "No son genios lo que necesitamos ahora," a celebrated progammatic text presenting the moral stance of its author, was widely disseminated; it was originally published in *Domus* in November 1961. I have written on this subject; see, for example, Juan Miguel Otxotorena, "La arquitectura del No o las grandes palabras y los viejos maestros (notas a propósito de Coderch)," in *BAU: Revista de Arquitectura* 8/9, (1993), 124–137

9   A 1998 manifesto, untitled but widely disseminated, referred to the state of Spanish architecture and was signed by Esteve Bonell along with 500 other signatories.

10   See the text of "Acto de presentación de AxA," which Introduced Arquitectes per l'Arquitectura (AxA) and was read aloud solemnly at the Barcelona Pavilion on June 16, 2011: http://www.arqxarq.es/docs/ActopresentacionAxA.pdf.

11   On this subject also see, for example, Terence Riley, ed., *On-Site. New Architecture in*

Spain (New York: The Museum of Modern Art, 2006).

12   See Mirko Zardini, "Dal Team X al Team x/From Team X to Team x," *Lotus International*, 95 (1997): 76–97.

13   See Philip Drew, *Third Generation: The Changing Meaning of Architecture* (London: Pall Mall Press, 1972).

14   On this subject see, for example, Bruno Zevi, *Saper vedere l'architettura [Architecture as Space]* (Milan:, Einaudi, 2009; originally published 1948).

15   See Peter Cook, ed., *Archigram* (New York: Princeton Architectural Press, 1999; facsimile of edition originally published 1972); and Dennis Crampton, ed., *Concerning Archigram* (London: Archigram Archives, 1999).

16   I have addressed this issue in, among other places, Juan Miguel Otxotorena, *Arquitectura y proyecto moderno: La pregunta por la modernidad* (Barcelona: Ediciones Internacionales Universitarias, 1989).

17   On this subject see Juan Miguel Otxotorena, *La lógica del post. Arquitectura y cultura de la crisis* (Valladolid: Universidad de Valladolid, 1992).

18   See Helio Piñón, *Reflexión histórica de la arquitectura moderna* (Barcelona: Península, 1981); and Helio Piñón, *Arquitectura de las neovanguardias* (Barcelona: Gustavo Gili, 1984).

19   See The Museum of Modern Art, *Five Architects: Eisenman, Graves, Gwathmey, Hejduk, Meier* (New York: The Museum of Modern Art, 1972.)

20   See Philip Johnson and Mark Wigley, *Deconstructivist Architecture* (New York: The Museum of Modern Art, 1988).

21   See, for example, my essays: Juan Miguel Otxotorena, "Dibujo y arquitectura, nostalgias y desmentidos," *EGA-Revista de Expresión Gráfica Arquitectónica* 14 (2009): 60–67; and "Arquitectura y 'blandografías': Notas para un debate obligado," *EGA-Revista de Expresión Gráfica Arquitectónica* 17 (2011): 66–69. Also see Aitor Goitia Cruz, "Soft Show," in *Actas del XIII Congreso Internacional de Expresión Gráfica Arquitectónica*, vol. 2 (Valencia, Spain: Universidad Politécnica de Valencia, 2010), 91–96.

22   See Ludwig Mies van der Rohe, "Bauen," *G* 2 (1923).

23   On this subject see, for example, María Teresa Muñoz, "Prologue" to Henry Russell-Hitchcock and Philip Johnson, *El Estilo Internacional: Arquitectura desde 1922 [The International Style: Architecture Since 1922]* (Murcia, Spain: Colegio Oficial de Aparejadores y Arquitectos Técnicos de Murcia, 1984). Also see Otxotorena, *Arquitectura y proyecto moderno: La pregunta por la modernidad*, and Juan Miguel Otxotorena, *La construcción de la forma: Para una aproximación contemporánea al análisis de la arquitectura* (Pamplona: T6 Ediciones, 1999).

24   See Manfredo Tafuri, *La sfera e il labirinto: Avanguardia e architettura da Piranesi agli anni '70* (Turin: Einaudi, 1980); and Manfredo Tafuri, *Teorie e storia dell'architettura* [Theories and History of Architecture] (Bari, Italy: Laterza, 1968)

118

OTXOTORENA

TOURNAMENTS

———

FELICITY D. SCOTT

AS A TITLE FOR THIS FORUM, the question—"What happened to the architectural manifesto?"—is seductively ambiguous: Are we being called upon
to reflect on the recent history of this genre, to examine or even clarify
what happened to it and why? Or, to doubt, question, or problematize the
continuing efficacy of manifestos by tracing the terms of their unfortunate
demise? Or is it rather a call to action, even implicitly a request to launch
a new manifesto, perhaps a manifesto about architectural manifestos in
an attempt to resist any such narrative of loss, an attempt to reinvigorate
contemporary debates by mobilizing the polemical rhetoric of urgency
so familiar from the modernist manifesto? This ambiguity calls upon
the speaker to identify from which discursive position she or he speaks,
a task that is less than straightforward given the convoluted topology
or interpenetrating matrix that has characterized both historical and
theoretical discourse in architecture as well as architectural manifestos in
the twentieth century. In other words, we might say, the ambiguity inherent
to the symposium's interrogative title reflects or reiterates the productive
slippage between modalities that has informed the field of architectural
discourse in the past and invested it with a certain sense of critical (and at
times political) urgency. For, on the one hand, we often find a manifesto-like
proclamation of contemporary stakes within historical writing, even if
not overtly taking the form of a declaration, and, on the other, a level of
historical self-consciousness informing architectural manifestos. This is
not, of course, to suggest that the writing of history and that of manifestos
have been (or should be) collapsed, or that they are without distinctiveness.
Rather, it is to posit the importance of the ongoing encounter and mutual
displacement that arises through their productively conflictual dialogue.

The question—"What happened to the architectural manifesto?"—
appears, additionally, haunted by the sense that something about the
discursive and historical context from which manifestos are launched has
indeed changed, that the heroic voice proper to the manifesto genre as it
drove modernist and avant-garde polemics, refutations, and counterclaims,
no longer resonates only, or simply, as heroic. Looming is the sense that
our perception or reception of such performances—whether played out
in oral proclamations, print-based media, exhibitions, or other forms of
actualization and dissemination—has thus been irrevocably altered. One
might, in the first instance, speculate upon whether or not this doubt has
arisen on account of the association of manifestos not only with progressive
tendencies but also with reactionary ideologies and forces of exclusion
and violence during the twentieth century. Moreover, in the United States,
at least since the early 1970s, there is the specter of the "tournament"

model of discourse favored by the neoconservatives and the polarizing, declarative polemics of right-wing pundits and demagogues to contend with, if not simply to avoid partaking in. But it is not simply the association with less progressive tendencies that has rendered the bombast of the manifesto troubling: if this were the case, Marinetti's "Futurist Manifesto" of 1909 would have been cast rather differently as a founding moment of art and architectural manifestos, or at least the championing of such heroism would in retrospect be more profoundly disturbing. We are, however, left with the question of whether (today) the heroic rhetoric and chest-pounding over heartfelt ideals now simply or irreversibly resonates with the dramatic prose of right-wing demagogues or, in the wake of feminist and gender struggles, with the machismo they identified at work within a largely hetero-normative, male-dominated field.

I would not, of course, want to cede the potential of launching polemical challenges to the discipline of architecture to reactionary tendencies, let alone to suggest that any such strategy was doomed to rhetorical cooptation by the right. Far from it. (The conceptual and theoretical register within which manifestos operate upon present conditions with some precision is one of the key weapons in the arsenal of critical practice.) In the second instance, however, as a historian, I want to ask whether we can identify aspects of the manifesto, or certain types of manifesto that might have lent the genre too easily to the foreclosure of critical potentialities and their recuperation as demagoguery.

Here I want to turn, briefly, to Charles Jencks's highly symptomatic endeavor to define the architectural manifesto as a violent, incantatory, sectarian call to order in "The Volcano and the Tablet," his introduction to *Theories and Manifestoes of Contemporary Architecture* of 1997 (a volume receiving little attention before this conference, in stark contrast to Ulrich Conrads's *Programs and Manifestoes on 20th-Century Architecture*, with which it was in explicit dialogue).[1] In his typically bombastic, ad hoc manner, Jencks characterized the genre (or, as he put it, the "art form") in terms of an emotionally charged, even biblical crusade bent at once on destruction of an enemy or outsider, the exclusion of difference, and the establishment of new orthodoxies. Manifestos "inspire fear in order to create unity and orthodoxy" he posited, additionally clarifying that it was the "irresistible display of violence and strength which makes the manifesto memorable and psychologically impressive."[2] Of their formal characteristics he noted that manifestos were repetitive and hypnotic, that they were magic words written on the run and exhibiting "an hysterical, telegraphic quality." For Jencks, it was the collusion between fearmongering—the "volcano" in his title, which referenced "the explosion of emotion"—and the institutionalization of new norms—its counterpart, the "tablet," which referenced the establishment of "laws and theories"—that characterized a manifesto. Concluding, Jencks tied this opportunistic logic of promoting fear to the once-utopian figure of changing the world. As he explained, "Crisis, or the feeling of imminent catastrophe is one more reason why the 'volcano' is as deep a metaphor as the 'tablet'—pure theory—for without the motive to change the world the manifesto would not be written."[3] What, then, we might ask, did Jencks imagine such fearmongering to be in the service of? What was at stake in such attempts to change the world, to establish new laws?

To be clear, I am not implying that there is something constitutive about the genre on account of Jencks's definition, but want to ask if there are manifestos that operate otherwise, to different ends—those that undermine or differently articulate themselves with respect to historical forces and political discourses as well as to established forms of institutional power. Are there not other types of manifesto, wayward versions or ironic appropriations of the genre? Or can we identify borderline examples that might have us asking: How on earth did the architectural manifesto come to look like that? Can we find examples of manifestos that destabilize the genre from within, even allow us to significantly redefine it? While not discounting the distinct possibility that it might even be Jencks's astounding ability to turn all polemic into pure platitudes, to subsume distinct discourses into his monstrous categories, which has killed the efficacy and specificity of the manifesto in architectural discourse, I still want to speculate upon other possible lives.

To do so I want to bring in three examples that do not appear in Jencks and Kropf's otherwise quite extensive selection: *Open Land: A Manifesto*, Leslie Kanes Weisman's "Women's Environmental Rights: A Manifesto," and Luc Deleu's "Manifesto on Orban Planning." All have an air of urgency and in this sense resonate with Jencks's definition. But in addressing pressing questions of their respective historical moments in the 1970s and early '80s, particularly environmental concerns as they related to the discipline of architecture, each departs from the critic's formulation in an instructive manner. To be clear, I am not putting these examples on the table as instances of more important manifestos than those included in Jencks's anthology, or as examples that answer my questions as such. Rather, they are introduced here because each one speaks, in a different manner, to the pressure of historical forces upon the discipline, as manifest in the manifesto.

Open Land: A Manifesto was not written by architects but by the communards of Morningstar Commune and Wheeler's Ranch in Northern California (1). It was, however, a manifesto about architecture, one concerned, specifically and avowedly, with the impact of architecture upon one's body and psyche.[4] While pervaded by the mysticism and problematic identifications often accompanying hippie culture, it stands as an example of a manifesto that staged a departure from extant institutions, as do most instances of the genre, but without indicating a means of return or of the establishment of a new orthodoxy. The Open Land movement emerged in the mid-to-late 1960s in reaction to what its earliest proponents—Lou Gottlieb and Ramon Sender (both musicians working with electronic technologies)—called "cybernation." Responding at once to the imminent possibility that human labor would be rendered unnecessary on account of automation and that those same technologies harbored the threat of atomic and nuclear warfare and hence a forced return to a pre-industrial condition, these communes adopted an ethos of "voluntary primitivism," a performance of survival strategies or anticipatory experimental testing of an alternative form of life (2, 3). Central to this testing were attempts to cede private property rights to the public domain in order to facilitate communal stewardship of the land. They hoped to make land available rent free for anyone to use, to open a space without governmental regulation. Offering her impressions of Wheeler's Ranch, journalist Sara Davidson recalled that there was a sign near the community garden reading "Permit not required to settle here."[5] Many had taken up the call to occupy land free

1 *Open Land: A Manifesto,* by the communards of Morningstar Commune and Wheeler's Ranch in Northern California (1966).

of charge, building makeshift structures or setting up temporary dwellings from tents and teepees to customized school buses and vans within this ambiguous territorial zone. The dwellings, Davidson wrote of the scene she encountered, "are straight out of Dogpatch—old boards nailed unevenly

2, 3 The improvised dwellings of the Morningstar communards tested alternative habits of living.

SCOTT

together, odd pieces of plastic strung across poles to make wobbly igloos, with round stovepipes poking out the side. Most have dirt floors, though the better ones have wood." The occupants themselves had a similarly poverty-ridden, even pre-industrial if theatrical appearance, wearing, as she put, "hillbilly clothes, with funny hats and sashes," outfits also described as "pioneer clothes."[6]

Exodus from official systems of managing land and the built environment—from property rights and trespass laws to building codes as well as health and safety regulations—was not as easy as declaring, "Permit not required to settle here." Indeed, the sign served less as a performative or speech act in the sense theorized by J. L. Austin (actually freeing the land of the need for permits) than it did as a polemical and political gesture.[7] And the local authorities soon fought back, giving rise to what came to be known as "code wars" and with them an escalating set of tactical and counter-tactical maneuvers between the commune, on the one hand, and local police and state governing institutions, on the other (4, 5). After initially trying to charge the communards with harboring dangerous persons, then repeatedly rounding them up and arresting them for health and safety violations, local government agencies eventually bulldozed the ad hoc settlements at both sites.

It was in this embattled context that *Open Land: A Manifesto* appeared in 1970, a text recounting how these structures had been a principal means for articulating and testing alternative modes of life. The "architecture," in other words, served as a strategic vehicle in the communards' attempts to withdraw from the state's regulation of the environment, as materiel in the battle over opening land. As more people arrived in the commune, we learn in the manifesto, "Sonoma County started a broad-based policy of repressions, including a punitive and discriminatory enforcement of the health and building codes."[8] "Even teepees and tents were disallowed," the manifesto reported, going on to note the county's acts of rezoning the properties, revoking right-of-way access, instituting new laws against the formation of non-normative households, and other tactics to break up the communes. The vehemence of the government's response itself indicates that at stake was far more than ensuring the health and safety of those adopting a lifestyle of voluntary primitivism.

A section of the manifesto entitled "Our Beleaguered Homes" further outlined their ethos of self-build, no-code homes. "How about building yourself a house? No, no, you don't need money, architect, plans, permits. Why not use what's there?" "[R]estrictive codes on home-building," the manifesto insisted in a related context, "make it just about impossible to build a *code* home that doesn't sterilize, insulate, and rigidify the inhabitants. . . So it falls down in the first wind storm. The second one won't. Dirt floors are easy to keep clean. Domes are full of light and air."[9] While the cost of materials and a

4, 5 Tactical and counter-tactical maneuvers between the commune, the local police and state governing institutions.

SCOTT

do-it-yourself ethos certainly informed the non-normative character of the ad hoc constructions, the manifesto reveals that the teepees, lean-tos, tents, open-sided A-frames, simple tarpaulins, treehouses, geodesic structures, vans, school buses, and brushwood hogans were not simply the product of a lack of building expertise (although this did of course often factor in).

Rejecting normative and scientifically justified approaches not only to housing but also to health, hygiene, education, sanitation, birthrates, and labor, Open Land communards were *not*, to stress, fighting for access to or equitable inclusion within the system. Rather, they were actively withdrawing from the institutions, practices, and sites through which micropolitical techniques of power had developed under a modern form of governmental rationality; they were withdrawing from the points at which that logic systematically met the body and psyche of the contemporary subject in their everyday lives. Open Land thus implicitly questioned the relation between the state's more benevolent role in ensuring the health and welfare of its citizens and the forms of control it exerted over them in the name of maintaining productivity, or more precisely, maintaining profitability for the capitalist machinery. Architecture, in turn, served as a tactical vehicle for testing the occupation of a counter-environment, tactical weapons in a war against the state's administration of dwelling (and hence of bodies) through regulatory codes.

6 Leslie Kanes Weisman, "Architecture as Icon," New York. The built environment as "a living archaeology through which we can extract the priorities and beliefs of the decision-makers in our society."

My second example, Weisman's "Women's Environmental Rights: A Manifesto," emerges from within a more specifically architectural context, but similarly recognizes, we might say, a matrix of biopolitical forces at work within architecture and the forms of life it sustains, reading them as "environmental oppression." Appearing in *Heresies 11*, a 1981 special issue of this feminist journal called "Making Room: Women and Architecture," the manifesto begins, "Be it acknowledged: the man-made environments which surround us reinforce conventional patriarchal definitions of women's role in society and spatially imprint those sexist messages on our daughters and sons (6)."[10] Under the subtitle "Architecture as Icon," Weisman referred in turn to the built environment as "a living archaeology through which we can extract the priorities and beliefs of the decision-makers in our society." What emerges in the remaining parts of the manifesto is a fascinating split between calls for reform to take place within the system through mobilizing architectural expertise—for instance, "We must demand the right to architectural settings which will support the essential needs of all women"—and something closer to the exodus of the Open Land communes. In the context of calling for the appropriation, alternative use, and even radical transformation of architectural spaces to counter social inequity and disempowerment, Weisman included a statement issued a decade earlier in the wake of attempting to occupy an abandoned building in New York's East Village on New Year's Eve, 1971 (7). It reads in part: "Because we want to develop our *own* culture... Because we refuse to have 'equal rights' in a corrupt system... We took over a building to put into action with women those things essential to women—health care, child care, food conspiracy, clothing and book exchange... a lesbian rights center, interarts

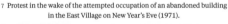

7 Protest in the wake of the attempted occupation of an abandoned building in the East Village on New Year's Eve (1971).

school, feminist school… For this reason we were busted… because we are women acting independently of men, independently of the system." At stake in both responses—the reformist and the revolutionary—however, and to reiterate, was a critique of the manner in which architecture served as a technique of power informing or sustaining particular forms of life. But there was also the hope that it could operate otherwise, and even serve to facilitate a type of disinvestment from such environmental forces (hence the need for the manifesto).

Third, I want to introduce Deleu's 1980 "Orban Planning Manifesto," a retroactive manifesto of sorts since it was launched not as a new polemic or to announce a change but to consolidate the architect's ideas from the previous decade. In this regard it belied the contemporaneity of the manifesto form. Deleu's manifesto returned to themes dating back to his earliest polemics under the rubric of T.O.P. office, in particular the limited land on planet Earth, the pressures of population growth and urbanization on food production, and the foreclosure of any remaining commons. In 1970, when he formed T.O.P. office, questions of environmental catastrophe and population growth were at the forefront of public debate, fueled by the survivalist rhetoric of R. Buckminster Fuller, whose *Utopia or Oblivion: The Prospects for Humanity* had appeared a year earlier, following Stanford biology professor Paul Ehrlich's best-selling 1968 book, *The Population Bomb* (8, 9). Also in 1969, Stewart Brand—a former student of Ehrlich and avowed discipline of Fuller—launched the *Whole Earth Catalog*, with a cover featuring an iconic photograph from NASA's Apollo missions, an image of earth from outer space (10).

8 R. Buckminster Fuller, *Utopia or Oblivion: The Prospects for Humanity* (1969).

9 Paul Ehrlich, *The Population Bomb* (1968).

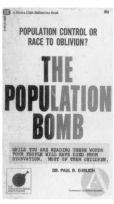

All left a profound mark on Deleu's thinking. For Deleu this new planetary consciousness meant that architecture and urbanism could no longer operate at the scale of housing or even the town, as he believed had characterized modernism. Rather, as he put it, "architecture would now have to be treated on a global scale." As he explained in another manifesto, entitled "A Task for Contemporary Architecture,"

The consumer society requires a different approach than the production society of the beginning of this century. The mid-sixties and early seventies was a period full of changes—social and technical as well as artistic. Le Corbusier and Mies died. The first communication satellites were launched, enabling us to see events from all over the world in "real time" on our home TV screen. Concepts such as "Global Village" and "Spaceship Earth' were in use. The concept "ecology" (thinking about the earth) was in general use by the time of the Club of Rome report, which emphasized the limits of the earth and its mineral resources.[11]

10 Stewart Brand, *Whole Earth Catalog* (1969).

Deleu invoked the popular duo of "World Thinking"—McLuhan's Global Village and Fuller's Spaceship Earth—on a number of occasions, making clear that what he called "world planning" or "orbanism" was indebted to both and hence inextricably connected to the so-called communication revolution (11).[12] He also repeatedly clarified, however, that orbanism was not directed toward designing or managing the Earth at a global scale

11 Luc Deleu, references for his thinking on Orbanism (including Stewart Brand's *Whole Earth Catalog*).

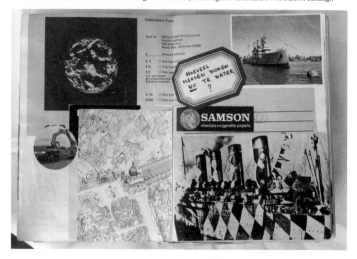

12 Luc Deleu, competition entry entitled "Mobile Medium University" (1972). This project—Deleu's first—was alluded to in his 1980 manifesto.

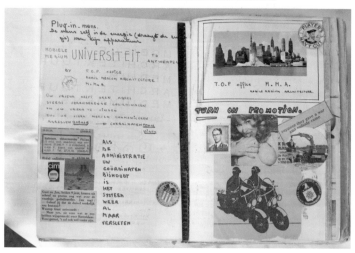

TOURNAMENTS

(as in Fuller's "World Game") but rather toward conceiving a model of design that was attentive to the scale of Earth and its interconnectedness. It is in this sense that we can understand the ironic commentary on global ecological interdependence appearing in two of his proposals. As Deleu wryly explained, "The proposal for an international compost heap in the Sahara is, for instance, an ecological project on a planetary scale. By shipping all vegetable waste to the Sahara, where it dehydrates quickly and becomes dust, the winds from the Sahara will carry particles that will automatically fertilize our farmland in Europe. I wrote a proposal to shoot nuclear waste to the sun. Obviously the sun is the best location to dump our nuclear waste."[13]

Suggesting that human settlement might shift from land to oceans, Deleu's 1980 manifesto alluded to his very first project, a 1972 competition entry entitled *Mobile Medium University* (12). The competition was launched in the wake of a decision to decentralize the Belgian university system, a move Deleu read as yet another threat posed to agricultural land by development. He responded via a proposal to situate the Union Internationale des Architectes [U.I.A.] at sea, to produce an institution literally traveling the globe upon three recycled aircraft carriers supplemented by no less than 33 helicopters and "communication media." (13) "A progressive policy," he explained, would attempt "to burden the earth with as little ballast as possible." In addition to such environmental claims were

13 Luc Deleu, proposal for the Union Internationale des Architectes (U.I.A.) on an aircraft carrier.

pedagogical ambitions articulated as geopolitical ones. "It seems to me," he remarked, "that a university that sails around the world with its pupils, connected via electronic media, 'diplomatizes' real world citizens, with an expanded view of the world."[14] In another drawing for the project, one ironically referencing posters associated with the occupation of the Parisian Ecole des Beaux-Arts in May 1968, we find the exclamation: "During my studies at the U.I.A. I was all over the world… I am a real international, not a consumers diploma!"

Deleu's choice of aircraft carriers could not have failed to resonate with their use in the Vietnam War at this moment as it spread into Cambodia. From aircraft carriers were launched fighter-bomber planes whose packages included not only incendiary bombs but also the defoliants and other chemical weapons responsible for the "ecocide" in Indochina. Such warships, if certainly abundant, were not exactly surplus at this moment.

The U.I.A. project formed part of a larger endeavor *Mobile Medium Architecture*, the manifesto for which appeared not in public circulation but in a private notebook in which the connections between American militarism, expanding communication technologies and transportation infrastructures, and environmental concerns, become far more explicit (14). After cover images of protestors, video cameras, and an IBM 96 column punchcard tucked into the dust jacket, we find a manifesto about mobility. It reads,

14 Luc Deleu, *Mobile Medium Architecture*, the manifesto for which appeared in a private notebook.

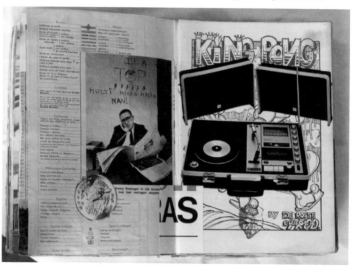

MOBILE
ARCHITECTURE
MEDIUM
MEDIUM-MAN [HUMAN]
_ Energy : -> Energy Belt -> Energy Clothing.
MAN + ENERGY
Can be plugged in to all media
- Minimize transport by maximizing [augmenting] communication
- Communication = transport x K
- Communication/transport = K

On the next spread we find *Mobile Medium University* in the company of two enigmatic comments regarding the communication matrix within which the new mobility, and the new "medium-man," operates. The first reads,

> Our friend has no address
> Always changing coordinates
> To find your friend
> You will have to communicate more intensely
> Address book -> CoordinatoPhone, CoordinatoVideo.

Stressing that such apparent liberty to move about is suspended within a regulatory system geared toward increasing control, the second comment, inscribed immediately below, reads, "If the administration keeps track of your coordinates the system is ever again worn out."[15]

I have written extensively about this work elsewhere, and here just want to call attention to two elements: first, Deleu's recasting of the name of his office (which stood for Turn on Planning) as "Turn on Promotion," and the launching in turn of a realized work, *Mobile Medium Architecture Promotion*, a customized Opel Blitz that appears in various guises in the scrapbook (15, 16).[16] It appears, for instance, in association with mobile homes, alternative technologies, and even a drawing that seems to invert Hans Hollein's *Rolls Royce Grille on Wall Street* of 1966. Finally, making connections to protests against the war in Vietnam, it appears opposite a photograph of John Lennon and Yoko Ono's legendary March 1969 weeklong "bed-in" in Amsterdam. If we take seriously the implied reference to Timothy Leary's catchy phrase—"Turn on, tune in, drop out"—we might speculate that Deleu was proposing that once a practice (like architecture) had been turned on to a new consciousness which, whether aided by psychedelic drugs or not, aimed to achieve a departure from conventional modes of perception, it could in turn tune in to the world around it and even drop out, hence relinquishing connections to the capitalist system and refusing to participate within its institutions and normative modes of life.

To some degree I think this is what is going on, but there are further complications when Leary's mantra encounters architecture. Can an architectural or planning office drop out? Is this not a contradiction in terms or even a categorical mistake? That is, if architecture succeeded in withdrawing from longstanding roles of environmental control in the service of capital and the state, would it remain architecture? Deleu was certainly struggling with such questions. In a text entitled "Spaceship Earth," he argued, "Urban planning and architecture are always a structural and three-dimensional packaging of socially dominant attitudes, and in this way the contemporary urbanization of the world (orbanization) emanates from the hegemony of capitalism, with its high consumption and low use of space." And it is here that I want to return to his "Orban Planning Manifesto," which ends by stressing that in an age characterized by massive environmental pressures, the critical task of the town planner-architect—what he called the orban planner—had radically transformed (he likened this change to the profound impact of photography on the pictorial function of Western painting). The architect's role, he argued, had translated into the dissemination of "information": "he is a medium, a trendsetter and/or town fool, etc... He designs, publishes, performs, shows, realizes or plays, etc." The orban

15 Luc Deleu, *Mobile Medium Architecture Promotion*; that seems to invert Hans Hollein's.

planner, he added in conclusion, "has become primarily a theoretician, who in rare cases realizes his visionary views on spaces of the planet earth."[17] As Deleu insisted elsewhere, he was not proposing that architects drop out but rather that they work in a conceptual or experimental register to launch images or ideas of a counter-logic, or counter-conduct, seeking to facilitate a critical self-consciousness regarding the discipline's relationship to contemporary forces, and that they do so in a manner promoting structural transformations from within the system, even as he noted, at the level of policy.

To conclude: in response to the question "what happened to the architectural manifesto?" I have not attempted to find an answer in a definitive sense but rather to use the process of questioning as a vehicle through which to articulate or recover the possibility of manifestos operating otherwise, refusing the normative impetus stressed by Jencks, and their role of "enforcing purity and orthodoxy." These admittedly rather marginal examples (and we might have taken examples instead from Jencks to make a similar point) suggest, for instance, the possibility that manifestos might

16 Luc Deleu, Mobile Medium Architecture Promotion, with customized Opel Blitz.

not only assume a strictly oppositional stance but could also launch critical contradictions that are not so easily resolved, particularly with respect to the process of gaining institutional power, or that even stage a tactical exodus from that milieu, if only momentarily. Could a manifesto involve the insertion of risk or aim simply to trouble, rather than staging opposition or taking the form of attention-seeking polemics? Can manifestos stress the articulation of aporias rather than claims of truth (something we find in the history of architectural manifestos but absent in Jencks's definition)? More particularly, I think such a process might serve to stress the need for new definitions, definitions that intentionally depart from Jencks's ethos of alarmist violence and the establishment of new norms. For the manifesto does seem, on the one hand, to be an archaism from an earlier period of modernity. But, on the other hand, like print media itself, it is an archaism that might retain a contemporary function, prompting us also ask what might happen to the architectural manifesto and how might it be defined otherwise, differently.[18]

138

1   "Unable or unwilling to advertise," Jencks announced of the impetus for the writing or proclaiming of a manifesto, "an architect must become well known in other media besides buildings." Charles Jencks, "The Volcano and the Tablet," in Charles Jencks and Karl Kropf, eds., *Theories and Manifestoes of Contemporary Architecture* (London: Academy Editions, 1997), 6–12.

2   Ibid., 7.

3   Ibid., 12.

4   This research on Open Land communes forms part of a larger book project entitled *Outlaw Territories: Environments of Insecurity/Architectures of Counter-Insurgency*, forthcoming on Zone Books.

5   Sara Davidson, "Open Land: Getting Back to the Communal Garden," *Harper's Magazine*, June 1970, 92.

6   Davidson, "Open Land," 92 and 96, respectively.

7   For an important reading of Austin see Thomas Keenan, "Drift: Politics and the Simulation of Real Life," *Grey Room* 21 (Fall 2005): 94–111. See also J. L. Austin, *How to Do Things with Words*, 2nd ed. (Cambridge: Harvard University Press, 1975).

8   *Open Land: A Manifesto* (Bodega Bay, CA.: Wheeler Ranch Defense Fund, 1970).

9   See "Judge's Ruling: God Can't Own Morning Star," in Unohoo, Coyote, and The Mighty Avengers, eds., *The Morning Star Scrapbook: In the Pursuit of Happiness* (Occidental, CA: Friends of Morning Star, n.d. [c. 1973]), 157.

10   Leslie Kanes Weisman, "Women's Environmental Rights," *Heresies II* 3, no. 3 (1981): 6–8.

11   Luc Deleu, "A Task for Contemporary Architecture," *Lusitania* 7, special issue *Sites & Stations: Provisional Utopias* (1995): 236–37.

12   On the relationship between Fuller and McLuhan see Mark Wigley, "Network Fever," *Grey Room* 4 (Summer 2001): 82–122.

13   Deleu, "A Task for Contemporary Architecture," 239.

14   Project text for *Mobile Medium University*, 1972. I want to thank Stefaan Vervoort for translating this from the original Dutch for me.

15   I want to thank Wouter Davidts for his kind translation from Dutch.

16   This reading of Deleu's Orban Planning manifesto derives from a longer text. See Felicity D. Scott, "Turn on Planning: Dreams of a New Mobility," in *Luc Deleu—TOP Office: Orban Space*, ed. Wouter Davidts and Guy Chatel (Amsterdam: Valiz Publishers, 2012).

17   Luc Deleu, "Orbanistisch Manifest/Manifeste d'orbanisme/Orban Planning Manifesto," in *Vrije Ruimte-Espace Libre-Open Space* (Antwerp: I.C.C., 1980).

18   The notion of an archaism with a contemporary function is taken from Gilles Deleuze and Felix Guattari, *Kafka: Toward a Minor Literature*, trans. Dana Polan (Minneapolis: University of Minnesota Press, 1986).

RETROACTIVE MANIFESTOS

—

ENRIQUE WALKER

THE TITLE OF THIS ESSAY—"Retroactive Manifestos"—is also the name of the first entry of *The Dictionary of Received Ideas*, a project I launched in 2006 with the goal of disclosing and recording the "received ideas" at play in contemporary architectural culture. Taking its title from Gustave Flaubert's *Le Dictionnaire des idées reçues,* this project examines design operations and conceptual strategies that have been used recurrently over the past decade, to the point of having depleted their original intensity—or rather, have outlived the problems they originally addressed. This essay traces the genealogy of one strategy—the retroactive manifesto—that over the past decade has arguably become a "received idea."

At the end of the 1990s, Rem Koolhaas and Hans Ulrich Obrist interviewed Robert Venturi and Denise Scott Brown. The interview text was published under the title, "Relearning from Las Vegas," in *Harvard Design School Guide to Shopping* (2001), the second volume of the Harvard Project on the City, a research project led by Koolhaas. In the prefatory remarks to the first question of the interview, Koolhaas claimed that the book *Learning from Las Vegas* (1972, revised second edition 1977) was the last manifesto and the first in a series of books on cities that imply a manifesto. In addition, Koolhaas referred to other four books on cities that also imply a manifesto: a book on New York, a book on Los Angeles, a book on Singapore, and a book on Lagos. Interestingly, in doing so, Koolhaas both identified a genealogy and placed his own research projects within that genealogy. The first three books were left somewhat undefined, but I speculate that the book on New York was Koolhaas's *Delirious New York* (1978), the book on Los Angeles was Reyner Banham's *Los Angeles: The Architecture of Four Ecologies* (1971), and the book on Singapore was Koolhaas's long essay "Singapore Songlines (1995)." Koolhaas admits in the same prefatory remarks that the book on Lagos was his own book, *Lagos: How It Works* (still unpublished), the third install-ment of the Harvard Project on the City. In short, three of the four books that Koolhaas referred to in his genealogy of books on cities that imply a manifesto were his own.

In the 1960s and 70s, the genre of the architecture manifesto came under critical scrutiny. Most manifestos had by then fallen apart, some as arguments, some for lack of evidence. In addition, the manifesto proved to be at odds with the practice of architecture, for a manifesto is elaborated before and independent of the specific conditions of a project, and in turn often clashes with them. Moreover, when a manifesto and a project do not clash with each other, the manifesto ultimately condemns a project to being merely its illustration.

It is no coincidence that both Venturi and Koolhaas attempted to divert the manifesto genre. Venturi introduced *Complexity and Contradiction in Architecture* (1966, revised 1977) with the term "gentle manifesto"—a paradox, for a manifesto is never meant to be gentle. And Koolhaas introduced *Delirious New York* with the term "retroactive manifesto," also a paradox, for a manifesto is never meant to be preceded by evidence, but actually precedes (and compels the production of) evidence. It is also no coincidence that both Venturi and Koolhaas had obliquely theorized "the brief," that is, the series of constraints that converge into a project and on which an architect usually formulates the problem that drives its design. Both Venturi and Koolhaas elevate that convergence of constraints to a critical position in the practice of architecture. In *Complexity and Contradiction in Architecture*, Venturi claimed that, since a brief is by definition complex, a project is by the same token contradictory. Architectural design inevitably entails the negotiation of conflicting constraints into a "difficult whole," to use Venturi's term. In the introduction to *S, M, L, XL* (1995), Koolhaas claimed that since a brief is instigated by others, usually a client or a competition, a project can never be the outcome of a predetermined agenda. For Koolhaas, coherence is at odds with architectural design, and the result of either self-censorship or cosmetics. In other words, architectural practice cannot be subjected to an agenda. Koolhaas had already voiced his skepticism of working on a predetermined agenda or manifesto, when he described his practice of architecture through the notion of a "surfer on the waves"—an architect can simply choose which wave to surf (and, of course, even if a wave is skillfully surfed, this would never redefine the nature of the sea).

As Koolhaas claimed, *Learning from Las Vegas* was indeed a turning point, and can in fact be read both as a manifesto and as a book on a city that implies a manifesto. *Learning from Las Vegas* follows the traditional manifesto form, insofar as it is structured upon the identification of a crisis and the formulation of a way out (which in turn is illustrated with a particular architecture). The book entails a critique of a generation of architects who had been trained under the strict design principles of the Modern Movement, but whose work was actually at odds with those very principles. These architects had been taught to produce forms that reflected their functions, while avoiding any resort to ornament. In other words, they were trained according to the manifesto-like maxims of previous generations, "Form follows function" and "Ornament and crime." The argument of *Learning from Las Vegas*—or rather, the implication of the argument of the book—is quite extraordinary. Arguably, the two maxims clashed with each other. Since form was to be produced as a result of function, and since ornament was to be suppressed, those architects usually distorted functional requirements (and in turn structural requirements) in order to achieve expressive forms. Venturi and Scott Brown coined the term *duck* to refer to those buildings that distort functional requirements for expressive purposes, and that in turn become ornaments in themselves. At the same time, Venturi and Scott Brown proposed the *decorated shed*, a mostly generic building that would address function (and structure) in a straightforward way, not unlike a shed, and would communicate by virtue of applied decoration. By embracing decoration again, and in turn by entrusting decoration to an envelope, architects could once more afford to address function (and structure) in a straightforward way, freed from the need for formal expression.

So *Learning from Las Vegas* does read as a manifesto, but as Koolhaas noted it can also be read as a book on a city that implies a manifesto. And indeed, the way in which the book is organized is markedly different from the traditional manifesto form, and is in fact quite peculiar. The first chapter sets out to examine urban sprawl with Las Vegas as a case study. Venturi and Scott Brown claimed that architecture had been unable to consider sprawl an urban form, or even understand sprawl, owing to inadequate means of representation. The term *sprawl* described an urban form that the field of architecture could not understand through its repertoire of analytical tools. For Venturi and Scott Brown, the traditional means of representation in architecture registered a *form in space*, but not a *symbol in space*. The question for the studio they taught at Yale University

1 Robert Venturi, Denise Scott Brown, and Steven Izenour, *Learning from Las Vegas* (1972), the Strip as seen by car.

in 1968 that gave rise to the book was to formulate new means for representing an urban condition organized by speed—hence their interest in the Strip and its signs (1). The book's first chapter produces an extraordinary array of documents that attempt simultaneously to grasp Las Vegas and to formulate new means of representation for potentially shedding light on urban sprawl (2).

The second chapter, though, claims that the book is not about Las Vegas, but actually an attempt at a treatise on architectural symbolism. At that point, the first chapter vanishes as it if were a "MacGuffin," to use Alfred Hitchcock's term. As it turns out, the book is not about Las Vegas or about sprawl, but actually about the opposition of what Venturi and Scott Brown called the "duck" and the "decorated shed." The "duck" was coined to diagnose a prevalent design approach among postwar architects trained under the tenets of the Modern Movement: for Venturi and Scott Brown, the conservative followers of the revolutionary pioneers. The "decorated shed" was coined to define a building type that would potentially offer a new lease on life for the project of functionalism, and in turn a definition of architecture as shelter with applied decoration. (Venturi would offer a technological update a few years later with his *Iconography and Electronics upon a Generic Architecture* (1995), prompted by a trip to Tokyo in 1990.)

As it happens, the decorated shed can be seen as a formulation but also as a finding, one triggered by the very material Venturi and Scott Brown gathered in the first chapter of *Learning from Las Vegas*—in

2 Robert Venturi, Denise Scott Brown, and Steven Izenour, *Learning from Las Vegas* (1972), new forms of architectural documentation for the unique conditions of the Strip.

particular their analytical section cut through the Las Vegas Strip, comprised of the highway, the sign next to the highway, the parking lot by the sign, the casino behind the parking lots, and the desert behind the casino. The *decorated shed* was the integration of these elements into a building: the juxtaposition of the (expensive) sign by the highway and the (cheap) building behind the parking lot. The renowned drawing of a sign on top of a building proclaiming "I Am a Monument" exemplifies the decorated shed (3). The building pictured, or rather, the building type, seemingly responds to the programmatic requirements (and in turn to structural requirements) in a straightforward way—whatever its program actually is—and becomes monumental by virtue of a sign that proclaims that the building (the shed) is in fact a monument.

The first edition of the book also contained a third chapter, in which (as with Venturi's *Complexity and Contradiction in Architecture*) Venturi and Scott Brown resorted to their own work to illustrate the arguments they had advanced in the book. The lessons they learned from Las Vegas—particularly their finding of the decorated shed—were to be applied

3 Robert Venturi, Denise Scott Brown, and Steven Izenour, *Learning from Las Vegas* (1972), billboard proclaiming "I Am a Monument."

4 Venturi, Scott Brown and Associates, Institute for Scientific Information, Philadelphia (completed 1979).

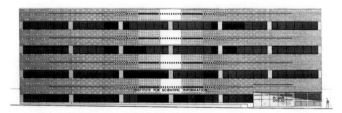

elsewhere later on. The boldest illustration of the decorated shed is arguably the Institute for Scientific Information (1979) in Philadelphia (4).

Not unlike *Learning from Las Vegas*, *Delirious New York* had a peculiar structure as a book when it first appeared in 1978. *Delirious New York* is a history of New York, though one written by following Salvador Dalí's "paranoid-critical method." Under the effect of paranoia, the mind is capable of mobilizing any information as evidence of one's suspicions. For Dalí, self-induced paranoia was an extraordinary tool that could suggest relations among objects that would be otherwise unrelated—what he termed a "delirium of interpretation." In *Delirious New York*, Koolhaas subjects himself to the claim—or the paranoia—that Manhattan was deliberately designed, that it was the by-product of a manifesto that, in order to be materialized, had to remain secret. What Koolhaas's self-inflicted paranoia causes him to suspect is a previously unformulated theory for Manhattan—a manifesto that promoted the intensification of the metropolitan experience, which Koolhaas termed a "culture of congestion," or simply "Manhattanism." *Delirious New York* is but a selection of the episodes in the history of New York that give proof that the city was planned and designed according to such a manifesto (5). Koolhaas traces this history from the amusement parks of Coney Island, where all of the techniques of Manhattanism were tested, to the tracing of the grid, from the definition

5 Madelon Vriesendorp, "Freud Unlimited" (1975), in *Delirious New York* (1978)

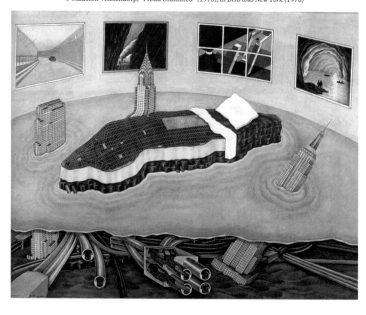

RETROACTIVE MANIFESTOS

of a park at the very core of the grid to the annexation of the grid blocks by buildings.

The key episode in this history is what Koolhaas refers to as "the reproduction of the site," the development of a building type triggered by the elevator. Koolhaas illustrates his argument with an image found in a popular magazine (6). The elevator fosters a new form of architecture based on the repetition of sites upward, the ruthless extrusion of all building plots. Each story becomes another site, one whose program bears no relation to the one above or the one underneath. Each floor is virgin land. What gives the illusion of a building is a consistent envelope around its perimeter. For Koolhaas, the inside and the outside become autonomous conditions, independent from each other. The epitome of this condition is Starrett and Van Vleck's Downtown Athletic Club (1930), a building that is indeed stable on the outside, and unstable on the inside—a homogeneous envelope and a heterogeneous program (7). Anything can happen on any floor: "eating oysters with boxing gloves, naked, on the nth floor" is the very description of metropolitan life in the Downtown Athletic Club. Interestingly enough, the argument underlying Manhattanism (the central finding of the book) is not too different from the argument underlying the decorated shed: the independence of performance and appearance, function and expression.

6 The "1909 theorum" depicted in *Delirious New York* (1978), from a cartoon in *Life* magazine (October 1909).

7 Starrett and Van Vleck, Downtown Athletic Club, New York (1930), in *Delirious New York* (1978).

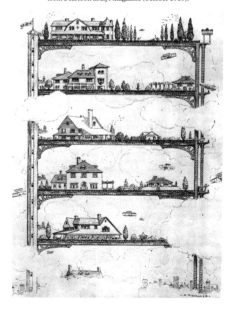

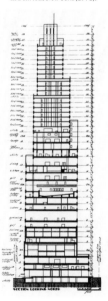

Just as in the case of *Learning from Las Vegas*, Koolhaas included an appendix to illustrate, through the work of OMA, the application of Manhattanism elsewhere. "The City of the Captive Globe" (1972) portrays a gridded city where each building is an extrusion of a block, and where each building, according to the doctrine of Manhattanism, celebrates functionalism on the inside and formalism on the outside—an architecture devoted to appearance on the outside, and to performance on the inside. The ultimate application of the retroactive manifesto does not take place in Manhattan, but elsewhere. In the competition for the urban park of La Villette in Paris (1982), OMA was shortlisted for an entry that overlayed

8 Office of Metropolitan Architecture (OMA), Parc de la Villette competition project, Paris (1982).

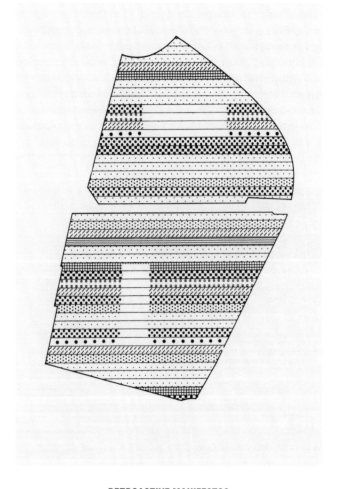

the section of the Downtown Athletic Club onto the site to organize autonomous bands of programs, including nature as program (8).

Ten years after publishing *Delirious New York*, Rem Koolhaas began a new research project. *The Contemporary City* (formulated in 1988) entailed applying the method of *Delirious New York* to the "city with no history." That is, he formulated a new retroactive manifesto for the so-called periphery—an urban condition which was deemed anomalous, and which in turn remained irreducible to the field of architecture. (Koolhaas strategically exploited the term "urban condition" to annihilate the difference—and most important, the hierarchy—between center and periphery. "Urban condition," not unlike our contemporary term "landscape," is all encompassing, and makes no distinctions). The project would also examine the most inscrutable forms of architecture produced in this city. As Koolhaas put it, in a slightly more polemical manner, it would grant "the dignity of a retroactive concept" to the most mediocre architecture (or "to each bastard, a genealogical tree"). The brief listed a series of cities, or urban conditions: Atlanta, Singapore, the Parisian *banlieue*, and Tokyo. The research for *The Contemporary City* was never completed, with the exception of the essays (all published in *S, M, L, XL*) "Atlanta: Journalism," "Singapore Songlines," and "The Generic City" (which articulated some of the findings from the research on Singapore). This project in turn led a few years later to the Harvard Project on the City (or The Project for What Used to Be the City, as it was originally called), a project devoted to researching the effects of modernization on the urban condition around the globe—that is, all forms of existing and still untheorized urbanism. In the very format of the Harvard Project on the City, and with the interview he carried out on the lessons from Las Vegas, Koolhaas honored Venturi and Scott Brown. And this brings us back to where we began.

The genre that Koolhaas described in his conversation with Venturi and Scott Brown—the book on a city that implies a manifesto, or the retroactive manifesto—is based on the premise that evidence precedes and might in turn promote the formulation of an argument. This is diametrically opposed to the traditional form of the manifesto, where arguments preceded and in turn promoted the production of evidence. The city, or the urban condition, is examined as a repository of potential architectural findings—arguments, conceptual strategies, or architectural types that could be appropriated and applied elsewhere.

The retroactive manifesto not only implies that the evidence precedes the argument, but also that the evidence comes from outside the field. From the sprawling city to the generic city, from the Strip to the elevator, from the gas station to air-conditioning, from the billboard to the escalator, this is *architecture* that the field of architecture had excluded from the field. In fact, the city of the retroactive manifesto explicitly *must not* have been preceded by a theory. In other words, it *must not* have belonged to the field. Venturi and Scott Brown claimed that *Learning from Las Vegas* was an equivalent of the Grand Tour, a voyage undertaken to learn from urban sprawl and the commercial vernacular just as architects used to learn from Rome. (This is what Venturi himself had done; *Complexity and Contradiction in Architecture* was retrospectively understood as the by-product of his stay at the American Academy in Rome.) But I would claim that *Learning from Las Vegas* and the retroactive manifesto are closer to the Surrealist wandering than to the Grand Tour. The city of the retroactive manifesto is, in its most radical form, not unlike the flea markets of the Surrealists—an irreducible array of objects, some of which might be appropriated toward a finding, potential evidence to articulate an argument. Traveling implies examining a city as much as diverting the material gathered while examining that city, and in turn diverting the city. Under the cobblestones, one might potentially find the beach.

By the time that Koolhaas and Obrist's interview with Venturi and Scott Brown was published as "Relearning from Las Vegas," *Learning from Las Vegas* had been disregarded for many years. At the same time, the format of the retroactive manifesto was starting to proliferate. Yoshiharu Tsukamoto and Momoyo Kaijima of Atelier Bow-Wow are arguably the architects who have since exploited its format and contributed to its genealogy with the guidebooks *Made in Tokyo* (2001) and *Pet Architecture* (2001). As it happens, the format proliferated precisely at the moment when Koolhaas identified the genealogy of "books on cities that imply a manifesto." Paradoxically, though, it proliferated at the expense of a key component—the finding. From then on, the format of the retroactive manifesto multiplies and mutates into books on cities that imply no argument, let alone a manifesto. Eschewing the finding, they become vast collections of evidence—books that capture entire flea markets. That is, the field of architecture has produced a large number of books that document certain urban conditions extensively, but without establishing a finding or advancing an argument. (Reinhold Martin has described these books as "books on cities by architects for architects.")

But let's return to the question of this conference: "What happened to the architectural manifesto?" On the one hand, as I have suggested, there is a recurrence of its "retroactive form," but rendered cliché—without the definition of findings, let alone arguments. On the other hand, there is also a

recurrence of its "original form," but as a kind of revival—without the definition of positions, let alone conflict. The question we should ask instead
is: "What happened to the advancement of positions within the field?"
Moreover, what happened to the advancement of positions that imply
conflict with other positions, a condition that was implicit in the original
manifesto form (and arguably in the definition of any project)? In other
words, we should revive the problem (i.e., the advancement of positions)
and question one of the recurrent ways of addressing it (i.e., the formulation
of manifestos). The latter is arguably a solution that has outlived its use
and seems no longer adequate to the problem.

151

MANIFESTO FEVER

—

MARK WIGLEY

THE AIM HERE is to quickly take the pulse of the manifesto in architecture, and to try to grasp its evolving role. A manifesto is a weapon. It is a challenge to the status quo, a call for action, a call for change. You use a manifesto to change things. But this is already far too simple, because a manifesto is not only a call to arms. It is also a form of action in its own right. The most famous example, of course, is the *Communist Manifesto* of 1848, but we could also use the *Anarchist Manifesto* of 1850. The gesture of making a manifesto is already a very complicated act, more of a performance than anything else.

There is no such thing as a small manifesto. Manifestos conjure whole worlds. A manifesto never simply appears in our world. It is a polemical document thrown into and against our world. There is always a violence to the throw. One world hits another. The violence does not come from force but calibrated disdain. The hit undoes the existing situation by treating it as unreal and unworthy. The manifesto unravels the existing environment without apparent effort, exuding confidence in its own better world. The manifesto has no doubt. It does not arrive as a utopian dream but as a sudden reality that renders unreal what came before. The manifesto-effect, the sense of encountering a manifesto, is the sudden sense of an undoing, the coming undone of what was taken for granted. There is a double act with every manifesto, the manifesto effect and then the effect of the manifesto, the effect of the effect—neither of which is obvious.

The aesthetics of the document are critical. The statement is always an aesthetic statement, even when the very theme is an attack on aesthetics. Indeed, it could well be that the act of undoing a world is necessarily aesthetic, even a rendering of the existing world as a form of ugliness or inadequacy. The look, texture, rhythm, sound of the document are mobilized and every element of the manifesto has to collaborate in a singular concentrated statement. The internal rigor of a manifesto is extreme with the subservience of all parts to the whole, no part subservient to any other part, and every collaborating point at the same level with the same weight. The manifesto galvanizes the aesthetics of horizontal order to disorder existing worlds. The anti-hierarchical document has many basic forms: points, principles, formulas, credos, programs, notes, demands, theses, positions, reports, retorts. There are many different ways to do it, each of which has a different kind impact and none of which is straightforward.

At first glance it seems like it is not so complicated. The whole point of a manifesto is that it appears uncomplicated. The word "manifesto" comes from *manifest*, "to be clear," so one could say that the manifesto form is about a kind of polemical clarity. It is clearer than any other document you can find. It is well organized, it is well ordered, it is compact, it makes points, it is super-edited. There is no word or punctuation mark in a manifesto that is not doing work. You could even say that a manifesto is a modern instrument or a machine, that it is industrial. It has a rhythm to it—tick, tick, tick. The points are numbered one, two, three, four, five, six. The relentless beat of this modern machine creates a sense of forward movement carrying the reader to an inevitable and better place.

But this sense of rhythmical progress is a kind of a trick, a ruse that crafts an invitation to blindly nod in assent. The manifesto does not simply appear in a particular moment and have a particular historical effect. Every manifesto positions itself in time, creates a sense of linear momentum, but can only do so by being outside of that time. The change it calls for is not a change within a space or time but a change of space and time. In the end it's not very clear who writes a manifesto, or who reads it, or even where or when a manifesto is read—and after all, what does it mean to read a manifesto? Can a call for a change of worlds simply be received or obeyed? All of the apparent clarity of the performance disguises something very complicated. What I want to suggest is that a manifesto is never simply *written*, and it's never simply *read*. For a manifesto to do its work, it does not have an author or even a reader as such. The point of a manifesto is to change the status of the writer and the reader. It wouldn't be a manifesto if, at the end of the day, the writer and reader are still in the same places.

Every manifesto carries a signature, although it cannot really be signed by one person. Even if there is a single name, that person will use the word "we." And the "we" is not the we of the writer, but the we of the reader. For a manifesto to work, the person who reads the manifesto has to countersign it, in a sense. The readers have to add their signatures by affirming what they read. And the manifesto is thrown into and against a space—so the signing of the manifesto, the throwing of the manifesto, and the reader's counter-signing of the manifesto are never quite what they seem. It is not a linear process. A manifesto does not simply ask for us to make a change in the future. Most manifestos are retroactive. Most describe something that has already happened. Or to say it another way, if a manifesto is a call for action, this action can come before the manifesto, during the manifesto, or after. It doesn't matter. Thus the great trick of the manifesto is that there is a complete disconnect between the call for action and the action itself.

In the same way, the action that is called for is never simply a construction or a production. The manifesto is always itself very well constructed, one could even say beautifully constructed, but its main purpose is a kind of undoing, a kind of deconstruction, a dissolution of authority. You cannot simply call for action without depowering an existing system. Of course this means that to make a manifesto you need to construct an enemy, you need a status quo—an "establishment"—that should be changed. Architects dream of construction, which already raises the question of how to write a manifesto for construction that will deploy a kind of destruction or undoing to achieve this. An existing dominant architecture will be visualized and treated as unreal, undone to make way for the arrival of the new. The new will move. It will be a movement. You need an image of something that is not moving in order to make a movement. So one of the first gestures of a manifesto is to stop things from moving, to make an image of a static establishment, then urgently call for movement—and making things look like they are not moving is usually more difficult than the movement itself. The real art of the manifesto is to make it seem that the world is still, waiting for the manifesto.

In this way the manifesto has to construct an invitation for itself. It has to create a space for its own performance. It could easily be that 90 percent of the manifesto is creating the space for the act. To produce the sense of establishment that gets challenged, the manifesto cannot simply be placed in the space of the establishment that doesn't yet exist until visualized by the manifesto, or simply outside that space, but must be launched in a liminal space that acts as a kind of incubator. The classic site for a manifesto is a newspaper or a magazine or a theater—spaces of negotiation and debate. The audience, by definition, is neither an insider nor an outsider. It belongs neither to the manifesto nor to the establishment, but sits between them in what might be thought of as a kind of democratic space.

This means that a manifesto is not simply launched by a new group against an old establishment. The manifesto actually creates the possibility of a new group by constructing the image of an old group. It creates an interior space, a space that you can occupy, by negating and working against a new image of what is said to be the old establishment. The call for action is launched by the innovative construction of a description of what supposedly already exists. Radical prescription is inseparable from radical description.

Now, usually there are no visual images in a manifesto of what is being rejected, or what is being called for. It is unusual to have images in a manifesto. Normally it is only words, but these words have been compacted into a kind of image. The manifesto itself is an image—its production is literally the production of a work of art. All the classic formal features—the shape, the typeface, the rhythm, the frame, and so on—are extremely important.

This is not necessarily an *avant-garde* work of art. The manifesto is one of the key tools of the avant-garde, and the avant-garde in its military sense might require this call to arms. The avant-garde needs the manifesto, but the manifesto doesn't need to be avant-garde and in a sense cannot be. It has a radical relationship to the existing world but not to the world it calls for. It's more like a stamp, or a seal of approval. In fact, a manifesto aspires to be semiofficial, even bureaucratic. It is a set of instructions, a set of rules, and there is no deviation acceptable. It has all of the roles of a seal or signature. The signature of the manifesto is not outside the document—it is the document. The document authorizes certain things in the world. Every manifesto, no matter how radical, aspires to be the law. This means that if there is an aesthetic of the manifesto, it is the aesthetic of the law itself. Perhaps when we think about the avant-garde manifesto, we shouldn't think so much about destruction but about projecting a kind of law and authority. Even the *Anarchist Manifesto*'s assault on all forms of government is carefully assembled as a linear argument framing key points under carefully organized headings that begin with the section called "Anarchy is Order."

Finally, no manifesto exists alone. It is always part of a sequence. It's not just points one, two, three, it's manifestos one, two, three. In the original sense of a "manifest," this document would be on the side of a ship announcing what's inside or attached to a public building announcing the new laws that have been passed. Literally each of these manifests would be placed on top of the previous manifests. So to read a manifesto, you have to read it on top of another manifesto, which is on top of another one, and so on. Manifestos are layered on top of each other, and each of these layers has its own precise history. The discourse of the new is always archeological. And yet you cannot write a simple history of the manifesto, since each manifesto is by definition a reworking of time and each mode of writing history has itself been impacted by specific manifestos.

The question becomes more precise when looked at with regards to ideas and representations of so-called modern architecture. Modern architecture is full of manifestos—they are everywhere. This should be no surprise, because the manifesto is the most efficient form of propaganda. It is itself thoroughly modern. It is reduced, streamlined, telegraphic, stripped. It's not by chance that the history of the manifesto coincides with that of modern architecture. It could even be argued that the aesthetics of modern architecture were the aesthetics of the manifesto, that architects tried to craft the manifesto-effect with buildings. At the very least, if you think in a more boring linear way about modern architecture having a proto-modern phase, early modern phase, canonical phase, postwar, late modern, all these different overlapping phases—the manifesto is always there in that history. So to ask what happened to the architectural manifesto might simply be to say, "What happened to modernity in architecture?"

The manifesto is all about reduction. It aspires to efficiency. Yet its length is not the key measure. What counts is how sharp the point is. In a way a manifesto is an argument sharpened to a point, so if you can sharpen a text, you can produce a manifesto. Each manifesto, therefore, has its own history of sharpening, distilling, cutting, cleaning, refining, and crafting the most perfect document. But even in the most reduced statements, there are never only the points. You cannot make a manifesto with "one, two, three, four, five," because first you have to say, "Here is the manifesto." There is always a frame to the points. "One, two, three, four, five" are not points, but numbers. For you to think of them as points means already that you have accepted the theory of the manifesto, and often the full force of a manifesto is established in the framing of the manifesto, not in the points it contains. We could probably play a trick in which we introduce new points into famous manifestos, modify or remove some, and nobody would notice the difference. In fact, this often happens. There could even be the pos-sibility that the strongest manifestos are the ones that can absorb or foster movement within the points.

Take the most obvious example, Le Corbusier's "Five Points of a New Architecture," perhaps the most famous manifesto in architecture, signed with his cousin, Pierre Jeanneret, who rarely shows up in discussions of the points. The manifesto was published multiple times, and the differences between its publications are a vital part of its history in the field. We should start with its first publication in *Zwei Wohnhäuser* of 1927, a book by Alfred Roth that documented Le Corbusier and Jeanneret's two houses for the Weissenhof Siedlung exhibition, commissioned by Mies van der Rohe. It is in the context of those buildings, and the exhibition itself as a kind of manifesto, that the "Five Points" appear. The manifesto gets a striking double-page spread in the book with the number of each point enclosed in a bold circle and the double signature underneath in bold.

But before the "Five Points" even appear as such, they are framed in a sequence of layers. First, by the book with its photograph of the two com-pleted houses on the cover (1). Second by the title of the manifesto. Third by the signature of Le Corbusier and Jeanneret, as already prominently announced on the frontispiece of the book: "Fünf Punkte zu einer neuen Architektur von Le Corbusier und Pierre Jeanneret." Fourth by the short introduction to the work of the architects that precedes the manifesto and the long essay and accompanying photographs that follows it celebrating the design, construction and completion of the two buildings at Weissenhof. Fifth, by the frame written into the manifesto itself made by a few introductory and concluding sentences before and after the points (2).

Two houses, two architects, five frames, and five points. We only read the points after seeing the houses on the cover, as if the points explain what we have already seen, as if the five points have been fused into a built image but can be separated out again in the text. The double signature is that of the two architects, again binding the architecture to the words and the words to the architecture—their double signature being doubled on the frontispiece with title of the architecture in capitals and the title of the manifesto smaller and uncapitalized, as if crucial but subordinate. The manifesto itself is experienced as the work of architects, an architectural work. What came first, the words or the design, remains permanently and productively ambiguous. The title of the manifesto has its own page with a drawing of the two houses underneath—as if the photograph on the cover is reality and drawings come between idea and reality, moving the ideas into the world or visa versa. The opening and closing sentences of the written frame inside the manifesto negotiate the uncertain direction of this exchange, hovering between the inside and the outside of the points. They point to the points that point to the architecture or, more precisely, point to that which can only be seen as architecture through their lens—so called

1 Cover of *Zwei Wohnhäuser* by Alfred Roth (1927)

modern architecture being in the end, and from the beginning, a new way of seeing things.

The framing text begins by announcing that "the theoretical considerations set out below are based on many years of practical experience on building sites." The points have been distilled from hard labor. They are the retroactive product of work rather than the proactive generator of work. The text ends by announcing, "The five essential points set out above represent a fundamentally new aesthetic." Modesty is never an option in a manifesto. Every word and concept is essential.

The five points appear explicitly inside a precisely worded frame. Even this frame is itself the result of editing and distillation. Le Corbusier had published points earlier in a 1927 issue of *L'architecture vivante* when he was trying to diagnose the meaning of the expression "l'esprit nouveau" that had been the title of his own magazine. He performs the diagnosis by using five numbered points, each of which is elaborated using a very compact clipped manifesto-like language. He is for "precision," "economy," and "clarity." He is against "regrets," "souvenirs," "distrust," "timidity," "fear," and "inertia." The five compact statements had formed the opening of his 1924 speech at the Sorbonne where they described the 100 images he presented of the shocking new reality of modern technological life organized into a visual narrative, like that of a film, as he put it. The rapid sequence of images accompanied by the sound of his voice reading the staccato points formed a unique manifesto followed by an extended

2 Le Corbusier and Pierre Jeanneret, the "Five Points" in *Zwei Wohnhäuser* (1927)

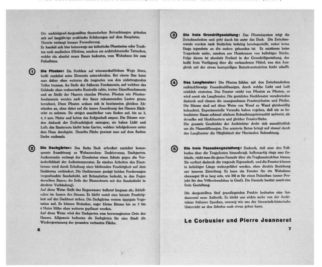

argument that was his attempt to summarize all of the thinking of *L'Esprit nouveau* starting in 1920—and in fact the transcript of the lecture was published in the *Almanach d'architecture moderne* of 1925, which was originally meant to be the last issue of *L'Esprit nouveau*. In other words, the whole body of thought that runs through the issues of *L'Esprit nouveau* is reduced down to these five sets of short sentences, which were republished on one page like a typical manifesto after a page of drawings of the latest Farman aircraft as the opening of the Spring-Summer issue of *L'Architecture vivante* in May 1927, just before the Weissenhof exhibition opened in July. The Weissenhof houses will likewise be presented as the latest distillation of all the lessons learned in the previous designs.

The year 1927 was the year of the points for Le Corbusier. He starts to be obsessed with points, and not just any number of points—five. Half of ten. It is a number that is connected to the body, as you can count it with one hand. If you think Le Corbusier's hand is not important, you're wrong. His hand appears relentlessly in his work—one hand. He is a one-handed architect. One eye, one hand. But in fact the order of the points changes and there even used to be six points, which were edited down to five. Le Corbusier originally had the "suppression of the cornice," the only negatively defined point on the list, and it oscillated between being the fourth point and the last one. The argument for the suppression was quite elaborate, lengthy, and important, but was stripped away at the

3 Le Corbusier, the Six Points in a lecture from May 1927.

un tel standard du cœur; de vouloir formuler un système qui ne serait pas équilibré sur les constantes éternelles de l'âme humaine.

Notez bien que ceux qui formulent un tel rationalisme suraigu sont eux-mêmes les moins rationels, individus mal contrôlés par une raison instable, ou peuples encore follement sentimentaux par manque d'équilibre. La « machine à habiter » est devenue la catapulte dont jouent, par exemple, les Slaves et les Germains. On m'a fait dire bien des fois depuis deux ans: « Attention, vous êtes un lyrique, vous vous perdez ». Et pourtant un esprit rationel m'avait conduit à quelques apports dont peut se flatter la machine à habiter :

Le toit-terrasse-jardin (¹) (recherche de technique pure);
les maisons sur pilotis (²) (recherche de technique pure);
la fenêtre en longueur (³) (recherche de technique pure);
la suppression de la corniche (⁴) (recherche de technique pure);
le plan libre (⁵) (recherche de technique pure);
la façade libre (⁶) (recherche de technique pure).

J'ai répondu : « oui, je prétends à faire des poèmes, parce que m'arrêter en deçà ne m'intéresse pas. Mais je n'admets de poème que s'il *n'est pas fait de* « mots en liberté »; je désire un poème *fait de mots solides au sens défini et groupés en une syntaxe claire* ».

La « machine à habiter » est sur le chemin de l'architecture. Elle apporte une solution inévitable au nouvel équilibre d'une société machiniste. Mais un équilibre social n'existe à vrai dire que sous l'instigation d'un credo, que par la manifestation d'un lyrisme.

Nier le credo, supprimer le lyrisme, est tout d'abord humainement impossible; et si cela était, ce serait priver le travail de sa raison même: servir. Servir à la bête, et au cœur, et à l'esprit. La « machine à habiter » ne marcherait pas, faute de nous donner la nourriture spirituelle.

Où en est l'architecture ?
Elle est au delà de la machine.

LE CORBUSIER.

(*Europaïsche Revue*, 1ᵉʳ mai 1927.)

last minute. Le Corbusier listed the six points in lectures in May 1927 (3) and all six were still laid out in great detail in the Autumn-Winter issue of *L'Architecture vivante*, with the 1926 projects for Villa Stein and Villa Meyer used as the models and analytical technical drawings included inside the description of each point (4).

In the process of editing down to the five points in the manuscript of July 24, 1927 that was translated in *Zwei Wohnhäuser*, each of the descriptions also change from a lengthy discussion to a short one. Then Le Corbusier finally published the five points in the first volume of his *Oeuvre complète* in 1929 in a still more compact form. Now that the points had been established as law, the frame is stripped away, although the introductory sentence about the theory having been derived from hard practice has now been absorbed into the first point. The most minimal version of the frame remains within the very points it framed. Le Corbusier has in every way become more efficient—which is not true of his readers. There is a set of drawings on the facing page in the *Oeuvre complète* that actually have nothing to do with the five points (5). They do not connect with the points, there are not even five of them, and yet architectural historians teach students all over the world that they belong together. The text to the drawings says in passing that the facade is entirely free and refers to the horizontal window, and you can see something like the free plan, but it is not described as the free plan. There is almost nothing of the five points there.

4 Le Corbusier "Suppression of the cornice" from *L'Architecture vivante* (1927)

So desperate we are for images that the drawings are often reorganized to look like five. The actual content of the five points is not nearly as important as the aesthetics, the appearance of system, of law. The classical aesthetics of order is displaced onto a set of five points. And the *Oeuvre complète* that now wraps the points clearly aspires to the status of law. The work is rendered as canonic, enabling the readers to feel unified. When Le Corbusier compacts the *Oeuvre complète* into a single summary volume in 1960, the five points now appear in parallel columns in three languages, reinforcing the esthetics of the law—even of the law behind the law—acting as a kind of touchstone of confidence for the readers who might even be able to recite the points, each known by the mantra of just two of three words.

The purpose of a manifesto is to create the sense that you are just about to jump off some kind of amazing cliff toward the new, but it is also to create a sense of solidarity. We will all jump off this cliff together. Or even, we have already jumped off. If you read a manifesto, it tells you that you're in a particular situation and you have a particular decision to make. Either you fly into modernity or you crash. It is too late—solid ground is behind. The language is that of imperatives. You should, you will, you won't. The central issue with the manifesto is always authority. And of course there is a very strong tradition of manifestos being central to the extended arc of modern architecture—and modern architecture was always interested in authority, CIAM being perhaps the most obvious example of the attempt to legislate the theories, set up in 1928 as a counter authority to the academic establishment that had blocked Le Corbusier's entry to the League of Nations competition in 1926. Manifestos have an intimate relationship to law; they self-consciously incubate law.

The examples continue, almost endlessly, and it's important to recognize that there is not an opposition here between the past and the future. Historians write manifestos. Almost all the great historians of architecture—whether Sigfried Giedion collaborating on "The New Monumentality"

5 Le Corbusier and Pierre Jeanneret, "Les 5 points d'une architecture nouvelle," in Le Corbusier's _Oeuvre complète_.

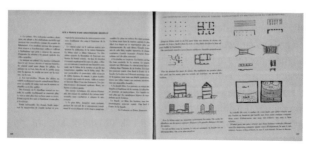

MANIFESTO FEVER

statements or Reyner Banham collaborating with the "The Non-plan"—were manifesto writers. Each manifesto constructs a gap between the past and the future, a kind of cliff edge that didn't exist before the manifesto was written, which finds the future in a polemic about the past.

This brings up the critical question: How can it be that an architectural movement calling for a new form of construction uses a technique, the manifesto, which is fundamentally destructive at its core? How are destruction and construction galvanized in the manifesto? The *Futurist Manifesto* of 1909 is the most important example here. Its celebration of destruction embodied in an automobile crash was first read by Filippo Tommaso Marinetti on the stage of a theater in Turin, reinforcing the idea of performance. There were some fifty Futurist manifestos that were shouted at theatrical events before they began any kind of Futurist work. More precisely, the manifestos were the work. A half-a-million manifestos were dropped from the Campanile in Venice, and another half million were dropped from an airplane. The manifesto is always performance, always multiple, always overflowing.

The *Futurist Manifesto*, as with its ever-expanding progeny, is not just about motion and speed; the manifesto itself is a motion machine, or a kind of accelerant. Marinetti said that there is an art to making manifestos which he possessed. He cruelly edited all of his colleagues and changed their texts—there being of course no difference, where the manifesto is concerned, between production and criticism. Manifestos are produced out of criticism. But Futurism, of course, puts us right on the edge of Dada, and Dada is the key example here because Dada can be seen as the art of destruction, the art of disillusion, the antiauthoritarian gesture *par excellence*. If Dada is anti-authoritarian at its core and the manifesto is an aspiration to authority, then we start to see the stakes of examining these texts. If we can understand a Dada manifesto, we might understand the architecture manifesto a little bit better. At first one might assume that Dada must be at one end of the spectrum—fully anti-authority—and architecture at the other end of the spectrum, fully authority. I want to suggest otherwise. Dada danced with architecture and vice versa—an odd but intimate and long-term couple.

The Dadaists would perform multiple manifesto readings and publish the outcomes in places like their *Bulletin Dada*, which gathered the manifestos from a "matinée" on February 5, 1920 (6). At that particular event, Francis Picabia's manifesto was not just read in front of the audience but was read by ten different people. The multiplying manifestos talk about their own status, even turning that talk into the main point. Here is the opening line of Tristan Tzara's "Dada Manifesto" of 1918: "To launch a manifesto you have to want A, B and C and be against 1, 2 and 3. You have to work yourself up and sharpen your wings to conquer and circulate lower and uppercase As, Bs, and Cs to sign, to shout, to swear, to organize prose in a form that is absolutely and irrefutably obvious. I'm writing this manifesto to show you that you can perform contrary actions at the same time in a single fresh breath. I am against action." That is the essence of a Dada manifesto—a call for action, which is the call to be against action. He goes on: "I am also for continual contradiction and affirmation, too. I am neither for nor against my own manifesto. I won't explain myself because I hate common sense." You use the language of common sense to say you hate common sense. The very last line is, "To be against this manifesto is to be a Dadaist." So, the reader is asked to not simply sign the manifesto, but to sign by reinstating that you are against the manifesto that you've just read. Only when you say you are against the manifesto are you with the manifesto. Only then you are signing it.

Likewise, Hans Richter, one of the founders of Dada with Tristan Tzara and Hugo Ball in Zurich, insisted that "Dada is pure revolt." The limit case of revolt is the manifesto. Architecture cannot be divorced from this. On the contrary. Not by chance was *L'Espirt nouveau* founded in 1920 by Le Corbusier, Ozenfant, and the poet Paul Dermée, who participated in that year's Dada manifesto blitz. Likewise, Richter, who would make films about

6 Cover of *Bulletin Dada* 6 with a list of Dadaist manifestos (1920).

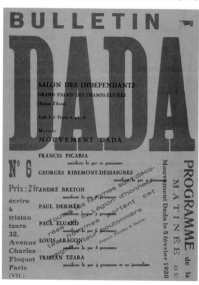

architecture and published a magazine with Mies van der Rohe, contributed to the architectural magazine *De Stijl*, which was filled with manifestos and linked to Dada through the figure of one of its editors, Theo van Doesburg, who was also head of the Netherlands Dada unit. In van Doesburg's magazine *Mécano*, of 1920–1924, there was symptomatically a manifesto in the first issue, and van Doesburg wrote many anti-art manifestos under pseudonyms in 1921, 1922, and so on (7). His architectural work and theorizing cannot be separated from these statements. This brings us up to the Surrealists, adding another archeological layer of manifestos: André Breton's "The Surrealist Manifesto," (1924) through to Salvador Dali's "Yellow Manifesto," also called the "Catalan Anti-Art Manifesto" (1928), with their ever-present concern with architecture. Soon we are already on the edge of the dissident Surrealists, the COBRA group combining the subgroups of Christian Dotremont, Constant, and Asger Jorn, who gathered together with a manifesto against Surrealism and against Surrealist manifestos and wrote extensively about architecture and even developed architectural projects. Constant's subgroup founded the magazine *Reflex*

7 George Ribemont-Dessaignes, "Manifeste à l'hulle," *Mécano*, 1922.

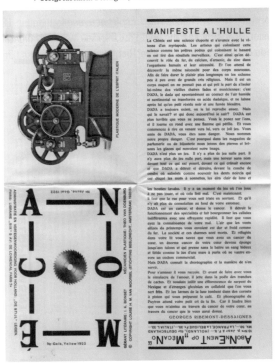

in 1948. There exists a photograph of Corneille and Constant reading their own issues of as if impressed with the work of someone else—this sense of the manifesto coming as a shock to its author, as if having written itself, being a key part of any manifesto's performance (8). Countless photographs show radicals clutching their manifestos, their radicality being an effect of the manifesto rather than the other way around.

More manifestos layer onto the original manifestos, and we eventually reach the Situationist International, which is formed at the intersection of the COBRA group and Guy Debord's group, the Lettrist International. Once again it might feel like we have left architecture behind and we are heading off deep into the world of revolutionary politics and anti-aesthetics. Wrong. The Situationists repeatedly identified architecture as the real battleground of their work, and of course held up Constant's New Babylon as the model of their project until he resigned. Almost every second article in the *Situationist International* is explicitly architectural and often takes the form of manifestos, starting with Chtcheglov's 1953 "Formulary for a New Urbanism," which was published five years later in the first issue; Constant and Debord's "The Declaration of Amsterdam" in issue number two of 1958; and the beginning of the first full explanation of Constant's project named "New Babylon" by Debord in issue number three, alongside the "proclamation" of the Dutch group; with issue four delivering the key "International Manifesto" of the Situationists in 1960.

Manifesto after manifesto emerges. Architecture without manifesto becomes impossible. The Metabolist group founds itself with a manifesto

8 Corneille and Constant reading *Reflex* (1948).

in 1960. *Archigram* magazine's first issue in 1961 takes the form of a manifesto. On the first page just the words appear; on the second page the same words are then wrapped around the images, which is an extremely interesting move (9). The statement concludes: "A new generation of architecture must arise with forms and spaces which seem to reject the precepts of 'Modern' yet in fact retains these precepts. WE HAVE CHOSEN TO BY-PASS THE DECAYING BAUHAUS IMAGE WHICH IS AN INSULT TO FUNCTIONALISM." That's a classic manifesto—basically asserting, "We are more modern than the modern."

Similarly, Superstudio and Archizoom are both organized around a manifesto. The manifesto written for the exhibition *Superarchittetura*, in which they first exhibited work in 1966, says, "Superarchitettura is the architecture of super production, super consumption, super induction to consume the super market, the super man, and super gas." (10) One of the most influential bodies of work produced in the postwar period comes out of this single manifesto sentence. Brevity is sometimes at the core of the idea—the shorter the text the bigger the claim, perhaps most polemically in the case of Hans Hollein's three words "Everything is architecture" in 1968 that radicalized the subversive project of their natural correlate, his tiny Architecture Pill of the year before, a "nonphysical environmental control

9 Peter Cook and David Greene, manifesto from *Archigram* 1 (1961)

kit" that could chemically turn everything into architecture. But once again this is not a small text reaching out to a big world, or even one author reaching out to a big audience. The manifesto destabilizes its author. Bernard Tschumi makes a decisive reflection on the necessarily masochistic relationship of author and manifesto in the 1978 catalogue of his exhibition *Architectural Manifestos*, arguing that the author is quickly alienated from the text and bound to violate the very rules that it drafts:

> Manifestos resemble contracts that the undersigned make with themselves and with society. As with all contracts, manifestos imply certain rules, laws and restrictions. But they soon become independent from their authors. At this point, a masochistic relationship begins between the author and the text itself, for the manifesto-contract has been drafted by the very person who will suffer from the restrictions of its clauses. No doubt such carefully devised laws will be violated. This self-transgression of self-made laws, adds a particularly perverse dimension to manifestos.

The list of architects from the postwar period who worked through manifestos and against their own manifestos in trying to reform modern architecture from within is endless. These are examples that need to be thought through because in the hands of such architects, images became an increasingly key part of the manifesto—as with the Smithsons, Aldo van Eyck, and Yona Friedman—not illustrating an argument but being the argument (11, 12). The texts have often been gathered without the images in books that become standard textbooks as if there had been no evolution in the manifesto form. Interestingly, though, those collections of manifestos seem to describe a period that has ended. Did the manifesto die? If the manifesto is so profoundly modern, did postmodernism mean the end of the manifesto? With Robert Venturi's *Complexity and Contradiction in Architecture,* it certainly meant the idea of a "gentle manifesto," but he would say he is not and has never been postmodern. Rem Koolhaas used the "retroactive manifesto" to be hypermodern rather than postmodern. The hard-core postmodernists anyway came out with their own manifestos—the New Urbanist manifestos being the most obvious example.

But now we are in a period of a super-abundance of manifestos. There are manifesto marathons and journals with fifty different architects being asked to write manifestos. At the Architectural Association at one point, if you wrote your own manifesto you would get a beer. That's sort of the ratio now—one beer, one manifesto. Endless books are being produced

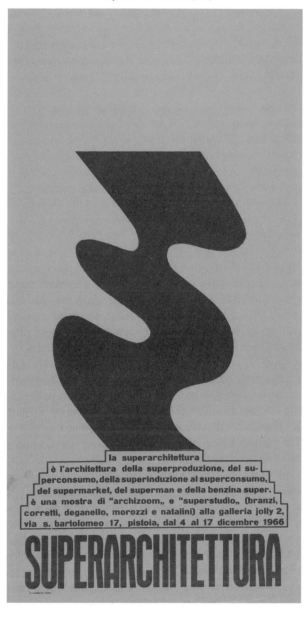

169

about manifestos. The manifesto is a document with no excess, hyper-stripped-down, but millions of these documents appear. In other words, there is an abundance of documents without any abundance in them.

So there is a continuous avalanche of documents that are trying to be deeply meaningful in ways that are absolutely uninteresting. This could just indicate that I am nostalgic for the arrival of the modern—the modern as the very sense of arrival, the shock of new things and modalities arriving. But I think the proliferation of the manifesto form as it's currently practiced acts as prophylactic against change—as if nothing will arrive other than the empty promises. Manifesto as weapon becomes manifesto as anesthetic. The strangeness of the manifesto-effect is lost when every architectural studio has a manifesto department or thinks of itself as a manifesto department. The manifesto is not something that can be

11 Yona Friedman, *L'Architecture mobile* (1956)

commissioned. It has to be the uninvited guest. What is going on now is that the students of architecture are being invited to produce a surplus of manifestos in a kind of parody, a massive unwitting Dada event of countless manifestos being fired off in all directions, simulating thereby that they are still trapped within a modern paradigm that has no impact outside schools. The machine logic of the manifesto they reproduce, the rat-tat-tat of words like that of a machine gun, hurt no one in an electronic age of entirely different rhythms where new kinds of performance will undoubtedly be incubated, new calls to action that reinvent those who make them and those who read them. Nostalgia for the modern manifesto might be the first victim.

ARCHITECTURAL MANIFESTOS

—

BERNARD TSCHUMI

WHEN I STARTED to prepare for this event, the first thing I did was to go to Revolution Books, the legendary bookstore now located on 26th Street between Sixth and Seventh Avenues in New York (1). I wonder how many people in the audience have ever been to Revolution Books? Probably not many. Once upon a time, many of you would have gone there. Revolution Books has many great and important books on politics, cultural theory, avant-garde theatre, revolutionary film, and so on, but no books by Beatriz Colomina, Peter Eisenman, Bernard Tschumi, Anthony Vidler, or Mark Wigley—by virtually any of the people speaking here today. Perhaps this is because we architects do not "do" revolutions. Le Corbusier said, "It is a question of building which is at the root of the social unrest of today: architecture or revolution." Le Corbusier thought we could solve society's ills through architecture.

Is a question of building at the root of today's social unrest? Could Le Corbusier be talking about the subprime mortgage crisis in the United States, or the nearly 10,000 foreclosure actions taken every day? How many architects were downtown occupying Zuccotti Park with the 99 percent? Not many. And not because we are the 1 percent, either (2).

Could it perhaps be because we are too busy creating pretty shapes and forms? Has architecture lost its social agenda? Like everyone else on this panel, I went back to Ulrich Conrads's famous book, *Programs and Manifestoes on 20th-Century Architecture*. I saw that almost every author in Conrads's collection brought together the political and the social, suggesting—or rather, shouting—that there is no avant-garde without a

1 Revolution Books, on 26th Street.

social program. It's important to remember the word "program" in the title of Conrads's book. Many of these manifestos are also about a new society: Poelzig, Loos, Wright, Gropius, Mies, Le Corbusier. Some argued less about society, but still included a cultural discourse: Kiesler, Buckminster Fuller, Pichler, Hollein. And what about Louis Kahn? No social or cultural debate here. Kahn mostly talks about design, form, and order. Theo van Doesburg also, doesn't discuss much that is social in nature; his first point is form. He initially argues for the "elimination of all concepts of form." I got truly excited here, but then he qualifies that as "form in the sense of fixed types," and goes on with a lot about form. Architecture, according to van Doesburg, must be an anti-cubic, colorful synthesis of Neoplasticism.

So, here we are: we have those who speak about society but not much about architecture; those who speak about architecture but not much about society; and those—the most interesting ones—who speak about both.

When discussing manifestos, Conrads's book always comes up. Why is that? After all, it is constructed in exactly the same manner as most other anthologies of architectural texts. Just look at the recent publishing past of this school—*Architecture Culture :1943-1968: A Documentary Anthology" after Architecture Culture*, edited by Joan Ockman; *Architecture Theory since 1968*, edited by K. Michael Hays; and *The State of Architecture at the Beginning of the 21st Century*, which I edited with Irene Cheng, in which we asked sixty architects and critics to state their own manifestos.

Even Charles Jencks did something similar to these anthologies with his *Theories and Manifestoes of Contemporary Architecture*. By the

2 "Occupy Wall Street" at Zuccotti Park (September 2011).

way, why did he choose the color green for the cover? Shouldn't it be red when you're talking about manifestos? And why is the announcement for this symposium green, as well? A shift from revolutionary red to peaceful green? Even among our major critical little magazines, look at the color and the titles—from the red-orange *Oppositions* to the white, gray, or black *Assemblage*, *Grey Room*, or *Log*. From a polemic to a logbook.

Where do manifestos come from? I went to Revolution Books to replace my long-lost copy of Marx and Engels's *The Communist Manifesto*. (Even the current Penguin edition has a red-orange cover.) The opening words of *The Communist Manifesto* are amazing: "A specter haunts Europe, the specter of Communism." The text continues by suggesting, "There we are!" meaning that we are already there, "already acknowledged to be a Power!" Now, this is speech and strategy: we are already here. We are already "a power." Imagine hearing, "A specter haunts the world, the specter of Parametricism." Actually, Patrik Schumacher, who is well-schooled, says exactly that when he gives public lectures.

But what interests me here are the following questions: first, do manifestos precede the event they advocate, do they accompany it, or do they follow it? Do you write the "Little Red Book" before or after you have won the revolution? Second, is the manifesto the product of a group, or can it be created by an individual? Conrads points out that the artist Friedensreich Hundertwasser was the author of the first entirely subjective individual manifesto. Now, this concerns all of us: you are a young architect, you have a few friends you like to argue with, but you are really on your own.

Let me introduce a bit of self-historicizing. When I first arrived in New York over thirty-five years ago, doing one-term stints at the Institute for Architecture and Urban Studies or Princeton University but really spending most of my time with artist friends at the Mudd Club or at CBGB, my agenda was nothing less than to redefine what architecture is (3). I didn't believe that architecture should simply be white Le Corbusier-inspired buildings or so-called post-historicist towers. I was writing and creating a 32-foot-long drawing on the floor of an industrial loft that someone had lent me. By the time I was invited to show this work at Artists Space in 1978, I considered it as perhaps breaking new ground. I didn't call it a "manifesto," but instead titled the exhibition *Manifestos* in the plural, so as to remove the pretense of a unifying theory (4).

3 Bernard Tschumi, center, after first arriving to New York City.

4 Bernard Tschumi, "Manifestos," installation at Artists Space (April 1978).

ARCHITECTURAL MANIFESTOS

In the little catalogue that accompanied the exhibition, I prepared a series of statements:

Good architecture must be conceived, erected, and burned in vain.
The greatest architecture of all is the fireworks; it perfectly shows the gratuitous consumption of pleasure.

Architectural space will be defined by ideas as much by real walls.
Architecture will be the tension between the concept and experience of space.

The paper representation of architecture will have the sole purpose of triggering desire for architecture.

In architecture, fiction will replace function. ("Form follows fiction.")

Architecture will break out of its cultural isolation and expand the particular form of knowledge of its time. It will both import and export.

New books will give imaginary architecture an existence and a logic of its own. In return, architecture will give books new terms of reference.

Architecture will not be simply the expression of accepted functional and moral standards. Instead, actions, whether forbidden or not, will become an integral part of architecture. As a result, conventional plans will no longer suffice, and new types of architectural notation will be devised.

Architecture will define the places where reality meets fantasy, reason meets madness, life meets death. (Border crossing is erotic.)

Architecture will be defined as the convergence of objects, events, and places. Such convergence intensifies, reinforces, and accelerates.

Manifestos resemble contracts that the undersigned make with themselves and with society. As with all contracts, manifestos imply certain rules, laws, and restrictions. But they soon become independent from their authors. At this point, a masochistic relationship begins between the author and the text itself, for the manifesto-contract has been drafted by the very person who will suffer from the restrictions of its clauses. No doubt such carefully devised laws will be violated. This self-transgression of self-made laws adds a particularly perverse dimension to manifestos. In addition, like love letters, they provide an erotic distance between fantasy and actual realization. In many respects, this aspect of manifestos has much in common with the nature of my architectural work: each of the recent works plays on the tension between ideas and real spaces, between abstract concepts and the sensuality of an implied spatial experience.

I didn't have to build—books were architecture, exhibitions were architecture, and advertisements were architecture (5–7). My work was about ideas and concepts; they certainly referred to architecture that could be built, but the work could also exist without building. It established a dialogue with other disciplines—with film, literature, and so on.

My concept-based work eventually led to the Parc de la Villette, Paris (1982–98), with its superposition of systems of points, lines, and surfaces; Le Fresnoy, Tourcoing (1997), with its facade-and-roof envelope; or the Glass Video Gallery in Groningen, the Netherlands (8–10). I considered each of these buildings to be a manifesto. Here, texts and words were

5 Bernard Tschumi, "Advertisements for Architecture" (1976–77).

Look at it this way:

The game of architecture is an intricate play with rules that you may break or accept. These rules, like so many knots that cannot be untied, have the erotic significance of bondage: the more numerous and sophisticated the restraints, the greater the pleasure.

ropes and rules

The most excessive passion always involves a set of rules. Why not enjoy them?

okay, but the building was a manifesto on its own. Each building exists to represent an idea, to develop a concept, to be a manifesto of sorts.

What about today? Ideological manifestos are rarer and more infrequent, except perhaps for green, sustainable, or ecological endeavors, but there are still other architectural manifestos being developed—some as in-your-face as those by the Futurists, others more subtle and more perverse.

Examples include unbuilt work by Philippe Rahm, François Roche, Pier Vittorio Aureli, and my own Factory 798 project, as well as several

6 Bernard Tschumi, "Advertisements for Architecture" (1976–77).

7 Bernard Tschumi, "The Manhattan Transcripts" (1976–81).

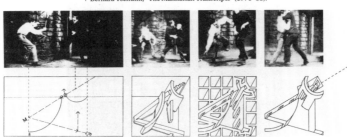

TSCHUMI

projects by other people in this room. And what about built manifestos? After all, the Barcelona Pavilion (1929) and the Villa Savoye (1931) were manifestos. And one could think of many other examples from the last ten to twelve years, in no particular order: MVRDV's Dutch Pavilion in Hanover (2000), Foreign Office Architects' Yokohama Terminal (2002), the CCTV building by OMA (2012), SANAA's Rolex Center (2010), Peter Eisenman's City of Galicia (1999–ongoing), and even MASDAR (initiated 2006), as planned and designed by Norman Foster. The list goes on and on.

8 Bernard Tschumi, Parc de la Villette, Paris (1982–98).

9 Bernard Tschumi, Le Fresnoy Art Center, Tourcoing, France (1991–97).

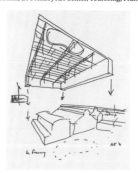

10 Bernard Tschumi, Glass Video Gallery, Groningen, the Netherlands (1990).

ARCHITECTURAL MANIFESTOS

Indeed, I would claim that any work that has a fresh, provocative, and clear content is a manifesto of sorts. Invent a concept, and it will become a manifesto! (11)

11 Ludwig Mies van der Rohe, "Working Theses (1923)," as printed in Ulrich Conrads, *Programs and Manifestoes on 20th-Century Architecture.*

We reject { all aesthetic speculation,
all doctrine,
and all formalism.

AND PROCLAIM:
ARCHITECTURE IS NOT ABOUT THE CONDITIONS OF DESIGN
BUT ABOUT THE DESIGN OF CONDITIONS.

ARCHITECTURE IS NOT SO MUCH A KNOWLEDGE OF FORM,
BUT A FORM OF KNOWLEDGE.

ARCHITECTURE IS THE DISCOURSE OF EVENTS
AS MUCH AS THE DISCOURSE OF SPACES.

ARCHITECTURE IS NOT ONLY WHAT IT LOOKS LIKE,
BUT ALSO WHAT IT DOES.

ARCHITECTURE IS THE MATERIALIZATION OF CONCEPTS.

CONCEPT, NOT FORM, IS WHAT DISTINGUISHES
ARCHITECTURE FROM MERE BUILDING.

ARCHITECTS DON'T CHOOSE CONTEXTS;
THEY CHOOSE CONCEPTS.

TSCHUMI

Acknowledgments

This book would not have been possible without the commitment and generosity of many people. I owe tremendous thanks to Mark Wigley for his initial support of the conference and of the subsequent publication. I am also grateful to all of the conference participants—Rubén Alcolea, Beatriz Colomina, Peter Eisenman, Héctor García-Diego, Carlos Labarta, Juan Otxotorena, José Ángel Medina, José Manuel Pozo, Felicity Scott, Jeffrey Schnapp, Anthony Vidler, Jorge Tárrago, Bernard Tschumi, Enrique Walker, and Mark Wigley—for their incisive contributions and their collaboration during the publication process. For their insightful contributions and criticisms, I thank the students who participated in my seminar on architectural manifestos in 2011; they helped me to advance my own thinking on the topic. In GSAPP's Office of Publications, Meredith Baber, Marina Otero Verzier, Michael Villardi, and Caitlin Blanchfield have my eternal gratitude for the hours they dedicated to organization, editing, and image rights acquisition. Finally, I owe a special thanks to James Graham, director of publications at GSAPP, whose tremendous generosity of time and intellect helped to finally bring this book to press.

This book emerged out of two conferences. The first, "What Happened to the Architectural Manifesto?" took place at the Columbia University Graduate School of Architecture, Planning and Preservation on November 18, 2011. The second was held at the Architecture Faculty of the University of Navarra, Pamplona, on May 2, 2012.

Published by
GSAPP Books
T6) Ediciones

Graduate School of Architecture,
Planning and Preservation
Columbia University
1172 Amsterdam Ave.
409 Avery Hall
New York, NY 10027

Visit the GSAPP Books website at:
www.arch.columbia.edu/publications

T6) Ediciones
Escuela de Arquitectura
Universidad de Navarra
Campus Universitario s/n
E31080 Pamplona, Spain

Visit the T6) website at:
www.unav.es/arquitectura/publicaciones

Produced through the Office of the Dean,
Amale Andraos and the Office of Publications.

Director of Publications: James Graham
Managing Editor: Caitlin Blanchfield
Graphic Design: Project Projects, New York
Copyediting: Stephanie Salomon

Translations for the English edition:
Martín Garber Salzberg

Translations for the Spanish edition:
Diego Galar Irurre

Library of Congress
Cataloging-in-Publication Data

What happened to the architectural manifesto?
(Symposium) (2011 : Columbia University,
Graduate School of Architecture, Planning
and Preservation)
After the manifesto / edited by Craig Buckley.
    pages cm
Papers presented at a symposium,
What happened to the architectural manifesto?,
held at Columbia University›s Graduate School
of Architecture, Planning and Preservation,
Nov. 18, 2011.
ISBN 978-1-883584-87-0
1. Architectural manifestos--Congresses. I.
Buckley, Craig, editor. II. Title.
NA2540.W49 2011
720.1›08--dc23
                                2014037090